What I Wish I Knew When I Was New

A Journey Into Youth Ministry

By Earl Henning

What I Wish I Knew When I Was New

Copyright © 2022 Earl Henning

All rights reserved. No portion of this book may be reproduced, stored in a retrieval system, or transmitted in any form or by any means; electronic, mechanical, photocopy, recording, scanning, or other, except for brief quotations in critical reviews or articles, without the prior written permission of the author.

Cover design by Earl Henning

Literary consulting, developmental editing, and formatting, by Clara Rose & Company.

Published by RoseDale Publishing
12100 Cobble Stone Drive, Suite 3
Bayonet Point, Florida 34667

ISBN-13: 979-8-9859515-6-1

Dedication

This book is dedicated to the Elmblad's living room carpet. You fought hard through our first years of home Bible study groups.

What People Are Saying

The guidance and wisdom contained in this book is a critical companion for any new adventurer heading down the path of youth ministry! Yes, it's more than pizza, crazy games, and camps. With his signature light-heartedness and humor, Earl gives the reader a true glimpse into some of the real experiences of a youth ministry leader. I've had the privilege of watching Earl's journey from a front row seat for over two decades and I can confidently tell you that his heart to see young people experiencing Jesus in a personal way, is unparalleled.

- Mike Nelson (His guitar player)

This book is a must-have for anyone in youth ministry. Whether you are brand new and wondering what you've gotten yourself into or if you've been doing this for thirty plus years (like me), you will gain so much insight reading this book. Through the pages, you'll laugh; you'll cry; you'll cheer, but most of all you will learn and grow. Pastor Earl shares his heart and his life, inspiring those of us who are passionate about making a difference in the lives of the youth!

- Kim Johnson

Earl Henning is one of those rare servants who combines an intense desire to light the flame of

Jesus in the hearts of young people, with relatability, flexibility, and joy in everything he does. Whether he is delivering the Word of God to youth or adults, mentoring the next generation of youth group leaders, leading his local community in service efforts, or creating opportunities for non-church kids to engage with church kids, his story will make you want to keep your lamp lit like he has and shine it's light on your body of believers.

- Chip Elmblad

CONTENTS

Dedication iii

What People Are Saying v

Acknowledgments xi

Introduction 15

My Church Background as a Kid 21

My Church Background as an Adult 25

The Shadow of Death 35

Nothing Left to Give 43

Ministry is 24-Hours 51

Time Is On Our Side 63

Build Your Team 73

A Little Help Here, Please 85

This Ain't Your Turf, Man 97

Oil Check 105

Comparison Kills 117

2 Feet a Year 131

The Long Haul 145

Conclusion 157

Hey, Thanks

What I Wish I Knew When I Was New

Acknowledgments

Hey, thanks!

Most people skip the acknowledgements part of a book - at least I know I do.

Don't get me wrong, I think it's polite to give a shout out to those people who made a difference, but I bet most people don't even read them.

In fact, I'm probably wasting time right now because you're already reading Chapter one. Regardless...

To my wife Nicholle, you didn't sign up to be a Pastor's wife and it's not very glamorous at times.

Youth ministry was my calling, not yours. You had a full-time nursing career with tons of responsibility, yet you went on mission trips with us, led Bible studies, picked up drunk girls from parties, and much more.

Thanks for talking me up and talking me down when both were needed. I love you beyond measure.

To my daughters Carrie and Lacey, you are both amazing.

You shared me with other kids when they needed me, played along when a kid had to live with us for a brief minute, and encountered endless things while growing up around, and then in, our ministry. You both served with me, dreamed with me, and cried with me.

Most of all, thanks for letting me always use you as illustrations in sermons. Well, you didn't LET me because I had a mic, and you didn't. You were always good sports and I hope those years were ones you'll always cherish.

To Dean Reule, our Senior Pastor, man you wrecked me, but in a good way.

I showed up at your church just wanting to play drums in the band and you somehow convinced me that I actually had more to give than just music.

You've pushed me, coached me, made me read books (which I hated to do), and helped me grow in ways I never imagined.

No other person has helped me discover things about myself and grow in my faith the way you have. I'll be forever grateful for you.

Introduction

What I Wish I Knew When I Was New

Introduction

Hello. I'm Earl. You've most likely never heard of me, unless you're a family member, or from my church, or you went to school with me.

If we went to school together, you're as shocked as I am to see me write a book as a *Pastor*. But hey, let's keep the past in the past. In fact, if we hung out together as teens, I may be just as shocked that YOU are reading a Christian book. Let's call it even.

Chances are, I'm a stranger to you, so why in the world would you buy a book from someone you've never heard of?

Maybe it's because I have the fastest growing youth ministry in... well nowhere.

Maybe it's because you've heard me speak at conferences and... but you didn't, because I never have.

Maybe you're one of the *tens* of people who have read a blog or two of mine.

Maybe it's just the title of this book that caught your eye. One thing's for sure, it's not because I'm well known or famous.

So, with all my staggering qualifications as a pastor, why did I write this book?

What made me think I was someone who could write

a book you'd be interested in? What do I possibly possess that could help you in your early years of youth ministry?

The one most valuable thing I have to offer, which only comes with time, is experience. Over 2 decades of it. And I should mention, at the same church. Yeah, I know, that's super rare. I like to think it's because I'm doing a decent job, but I think our Senior Pastor just knows it's easier than training someone new.

Either way, here we are. Just you and me. Two people who had some crazy desire to work with young people. People with a craving to see a new generation experience the grace and love of a God we have encountered somewhere along the way in our own lives.

It's exciting, right? I mean the idea of using your gifting to make an eternal difference. To serve Jesus by serving others and maybe even get a paycheck for it if you're lucky.

Lock-ins, pizza parties, laughter, messy games, bowling, laughter, standing on the big stage sharing your Yoda-like wisdom to the spiritually starved crowd, and more laughter!

All of that is... well... not what real youth ministry is at all. At least not what I've come to believe over my years.

Don't get me wrong, it's part of it, a large percentage of it. But if that was the pitch you got when you were offered this role, there was some really important stuff missing.

Stuff I was never prepared for. Stuff I never wanted, and stuff I never want to experience again. Stuff, that by year two had me saying, "I wonder if Home Depot is hiring? I think I'd look good in a smock, and I like the smell of mulch better than Middle Schoolers."

I'm not trying to scare you. I'm not trying to talk you out of ministry, or make you second guess your decision to jump in this thing.

I think Bill Hybels said it best when he stated, "The local church is the hope of the world." I believe that and agree with all my heart.

What we've been assigned to do in this season of our life, is humbling and insanely important. I just don't want you to be caught off guard in your early years, by the intensity of some things no one seems to put in the job description.

Honestly, it isn't being talked about in most books I've read in my career. And I've read a bunch of 'em.

I've read how to recruit a team, design logos, prepare a sermon, craft small groups, and even the best method for deciding how many pizzas to order. I swear that's true. It was actually in a book. Oh, and it's by the slice, not the whole pie. *Think 2 slices per person, then do the math with your local pizza joint salesperson.*

So, to wrap up this whole introduction thing and get to the real meat of it; the whole reason I decided to write this book was to simply help new, young leaders be strong out of the gate, and *stay* strong.

I have seen the rewards of being in it for the long haul, and I want to do my part to ensure others see the same payoff.

But just remember:

It can be hard.

It can be taxing.

It can be frustrating.

But it's worth it.

Let's get started, shall we?

My Church Background As A Kid

What I Wish I Knew When I Was New

Chapter 1
My Church Background as a Kid

I had none.

What I Wish I Knew When I Was New

My Church Background As An Adult

Chapter 2
My Church Background as an Adult

My intention isn't to give you my testimony or whole life story, but I think it's important for you to know at least a little bit about how I got to where I am at the time of writing this.

So, as you read in Chapter 1, I had no church background as a kid. It's just something we didn't do. Not because of bad feelings towards it or bad experiences. My parents weren't atheists or Scientologists, we just didn't do the church thing.

Fast forward to my early 20's. My wife, Nicholle, and I had moved to a little town, and she decided we were going to bring our oldest daughter to VBS (whatever that was) at a small church down the street.

She also decided that "we" were going to start attending Sunday services. I told her to have fun and I'd see her when she got home. I just wasn't interested.

That lasted a couple of weeks until I felt guilty and went with her. She then, so graciously, told the Pastor that I would audition for the open drummer spot in the new "contemporary service" (again, whatever that was). I was angry. But hey, a musician will use any outlet they can to showcase their self-proclaimed mad skills. Besides, three years of living in an apartment and not having my drums set up was killing me.

I agreed and was given a cassette to practice from (ask your parents what a cassette is if needed). It included the song "Flood" by an ancient band named Jars of Clay and I gotta say, it wasn't terrible. In fact, it kind of *rocked*, if I can say that about Christian music. I didn't even know there *was* such a thing as Christian music much less a rock version of it. So, it worked for me.

Time passed, I played, I sang, I listened to the sermons, and I grew. I grew a lot. My new-found faith was fulfilling and fun, and honestly, shocking. Luckily, Nicholle knew what was best for our family and to this day I'm grateful that she led the way.

I never imagined this for my life. And not only that, but now I was convinced I was on track to becoming a famous Christian music artist, as my buddies Mike and Colin and I began to write, record, and even get a little radio time.

It was all making sense now! This is what God had been leading me up to! I actually *was* going to be the rockstar I always dreamed of being since childhood, but just... holier, I guess.

Just a few years into our first church experience, the "more mature in age" crowd had decided they'd had enough of the energetic young Pastor they had brought in, and they loathed looking at drums on the stage. True story, they actually made him cover the drums with a sheet for their "traditional service" (whatever that was).

Fast forward again. My wife and two daughters, as well as my buddy Mike, ended up at a new church, and I was suddenly asked to *oversee the worship band*. I knew very little about leading any kind of team, but hey, why not? Music was my life, and I took every opportunity to use it, and now in this new journey of mine, to serve Jesus with it. Plus, it would keep Mike and I fresh while we waited for our record deal to come through. Spoiler alert! It never did.

Mohawks, Music, and Ministry

I was 29 years old and loving life. We adored our new church and were serving with more passion than ever imagined. While leading the worship team, I sported a clean-shaven head and would occasionally rock a low profile mohawk, usually dyed a color to fit the holiday season.

There were 8 kids in the youth ministry at the time and much to my dismay, they took a liking to me. *The-new-drummer-with-the-colored-mohawk* moniker seemed to confuse them into thinking I wanted to be around teenagers. But surprisingly, they were pretty fun to talk to every Sunday. They introduced me to new bands, listened to my dumb stories about *when I was your age*, and seemed to start seeking me out even just to talk about life stuff. Plus, they thought I was super cool and funny. Who doesn't want that kind of affirmation in their life?

I was completely oblivious to what God was up to, but shortly, I would get it.

The couple who was leading the youth program decided it was time for them to step back and pursue other things. So, who do you think the church leaders came to as the next sucker...? I mean, volunteer replacement. Yep. I really didn't want to. Like, not at all. At least I tried to tell myself that. I had no experience, I didn't really like kids, and I was still somewhat newer in my faith. I still thought *Job* was pronounced like the thing that gave you a paycheck every week.

Can I share an even more embarrassing piece of evidence which proves I was not qualified to lead a generation to Jesus?

As a gift from my mother-in-law, I had received the Bible on cassette tape. I almost returned it to the bookstore because I was convinced, they were trying to rip us off. I mean, these four tapes (known as The Gospels) all had the same stories on them!

I heard that he was born of a virgin already! That's the same blind guy from the other one I listened to! I thought they had just dubbed the same stories on each one and gave them different titles thinking no one would notice.

Keep in mind I had never even cracked open an actual Bible and read the Gospels. Luckily, I figured it out before the humiliation of a trip to the bookstore, to ream out some poor guy who just worked part-time to get through college or something.

"Sure, I'll do it."

I have no idea why I agreed, but I think it's because it sounded fun. They would tell me about their trips to concerts, pizza nights, crazy games, and TPing the Children's Pastor's house. Heck yeah, I'm down for that! I get to act like I'm in High School again and people *expect* it? Sign me up!

The group began to grow and in just a few months the church offered to pay me as a part-timer. I thought, *Hang on. You're gonna give me money to do this stuff? This can't be real.*

But it was, and it was awesome. I was leading the worship team and youth simultaneously for a while, until I was confronted with the most challenging decision to ever stare me in the face.

Talking it or walking it?

I was asked to meet with our Lead Pastor and a guy named Chip.

Chip was on the worship team; he was also one of the church's Senior Leaders and had three kids in the youth program. We'd gotten to know each other well and these were two guys I admired and respected more than almost anyone I had ever known.

"We want you to come full time with the youth at the church." I truly wasn't expecting that.

I mean, yes, I had started feeling like God may have more for me than what I was currently doing full time at the mail-order pharmacy and yes, I had begun praying for Him to open new doors for me. I just didn't think anything would actually happen.

If anything *would happen*, I expected it to be in music. I told them, "I think you've got the wrong guy," in my very Moses, Exodus, Chapter 3 and 4 kind of way.

I had no seminary training, no experience, little Bible knowledge and wasn't even sure how into this youth thing I was, especially long-term. I was kind of… in shock. I didn't even know how to answer, and I didn't for a few days.

Most people would jump on an opportunity like that, but this was potentially a dangerous decision to make. There was a lot riding on it and to be candid, I was scared.

It was not in an audible voice, but I heard God ask, "Do you really have the kind of faith you say you do? Are you gonna walk it or just talk it?"

With incredible apprehension, on April 8th, 2003, I accepted the offer. I left a steady job of 12 years, with a benefit package that would make you throw up if you heard how amazing it was.

What did I leave for? A young, small church of maybe 100 people, who met in a movie theater. Less pay, no benefits, and no guarantee of how long this church would even last. Only Christians do this kind of thing, I think.

But what if it backfired? What if I chose wrong and my family suffered because of my selfishness to seek bigger things? What if it was the devil's voice and not God's? What if, what if, what if? For the first time in my life, I began to struggle with my own confidence and abilities. I knew I wasn't qualified for this, and I wasn't sure I was even ready.

I wasn't.

Let's wrap this up and move on already

I had no idea what this role entailed outside of the games, concerts, pizza, and typical youth group antics. But things got real in a hurry and my already shaky confidence was pummeled over and over, with things no one had prepared me for.

The strain on your own family, the struggle to please everyone when you know nothing, the strong emotional connections you develop with the kids and families you serve, the danger of comparisons, the feelings of failure, time and time again. I could dedicate a thousand chapters to a thousand things.

It was blindsiding and it was hard. But what I have gleaned from 20+ years is that this was *also* youth ministry, like it or not. It can sound deflating, negative, and intimidating if it's communicated the wrong way.

My hope, in the remaining chapters of this book, is to illuminate the tough stuff in a way that just gets you ready.

My desire is that after year one, year two, and year three, you will still be as energized to lead and serve as when you got the job offer.

I hope, one day, you will pass this book on to the new youth leader down the street, who is as clueless as we all were at one point and say, "Here's some insider info that you wanna know."

I'm hoping to prepare you to work through the grueling tasks of this amazing calling on our lives, more easily.

Preparation is everything!

"Give me six hours to chop down a tree and I will spend the first four sharpening the axe."

— Abraham Lincoln

THE SHADOW OF DEATH

What I Wish I Knew When I Was New

Chapter 3
The Shadow of Death

I want to warn you right now, this chapter is the hardest for me to write and might be the hardest for people to read. It's dark, depressing, and heavy.

That's why I want to get it out of the way first. Plus, this was the thing I struggled with the most. What I've learned from other people in ministry is that I'm not alone. Everyone I know has dealt with this and I pray you will be the exception.

It was somewhere in between the first and second year of my part-time run as the youth Pastor. A young lady, 16 years old, was having her tonsils removed. Simple, common... usually.

I received a phone call that I needed to get down to the hospital immediately. It's a rare event, but she had developed an infection and had gone septic. The prognosis was, she was failing fast. I jumped in my car, heart pounding, and sped up to the hospital.

As I ran up the hospital sidewalk, a gentleman from our church met me and said, "She's gone." I felt my whole body go cold and I began trembling.

Entering the floor she was on, I saw her father, sitting with his head in his hands uncontrollably sobbing. Her brother was there, who was also in our youth ministry, as well as other family and friends.

The air felt physically thick. Everything was so chaotic and somber. I had never experienced anything like it. I didn't know what to say or do. How do I help here? I felt powerless.

A couple of days went by, and I was really having a tough time processing what had happened. Our group was small at the time, maybe 10 kids, so they were all remarkably close.

I remember a mom of another girl in the group calling me and saying, "I think you should get the kids together and talk about this. They need you right now."

I had no idea what I was supposed to say. None of the youth ministry books I had read had a chapter called *What to do when the superstar of your youth group passes away*. So, I gathered as many Bible verses as I could about death and the brilliance of Heaven. I prepared some things to say about *being in a better place* and *God is still good*.

But as the kids arrived, I quickly realized that they didn't want Bible verses, at least not right now. They didn't want a makeshift eulogy or someone to convince them that this was just *God's plan*. More than answers, what they wanted was each other.

They just wanted to sit as a church family and cry together. They wanted to talk about what she meant to them and share a story or two.

Some didn't say a word, but just sat with their head on the shoulder of the person next to them. What was *my* role? Just bring them together. To give them an outlet and remind them they were not alone, and that I was struggling just as much as they were.

That moment taught me the importance of that thing they call the *be there, factor*. It's more powerful than theology, more effective than 3 years of Bible school and sticks in the minds of our students longer than any sermon I gave. Good thing, because, unfortunately, this wouldn't be the only time I would need it.

The Hits Just Keep on Coming

I wish that were the only event of its kind. Not even close. Again, I want to warn you about the heaviness of what you're about to read. This was my reality and it's the only reason I'm putting them in here. Someone has to say it.

A few years after the first tragedy, came another. I remember it vividly. It was a few days before Christmas and I was walking through JCPenney with my family, when my phone rang. It was a student in our group, hysterically crying.

She informed me that a family of four were all killed when their private plane went down as they went to visit family. Their two daughters were both in our youth group and all four were heavily involved in our church.

Our Senior Pastor was out of town for the holidays, and I was hit with the same words as the first time I encountered this. *They need you right now*.

I was asked to host a memorial service for the local friends and family. This may not catch you by surprise, but I had never done one before. What do I do? What do I say? Am I really responsible for trying to bring comfort and peace to others when I'm struggling to find it myself?

But I did it. And I hated it.

This was just another chapter that was not in any of my youth ministry books and another role that wasn't in my job description.

Fast forward in my career to a machine gun onslaught of unwanted on-the-job training, I was unprepared and unqualified to handle.

I received a text one morning from a young man which simply read, "My father is dead."

He had found him on the kitchen floor that morning and tried to revive him. He showed up at Bible Study that night because he said he *needed to be around his people.*

A couple of years later, I received a call that four siblings in our group had just lost their father in an extremely dramatic white-water rafting accident. The mother asked me to come sit at the table while she broke the news to them.

Yep. Not kidding. Absolutely the most horrible thing I've ever had to witness. I never wanted to go through that again.

But... I got another call. The father of more siblings in our group had just taken his own life, and the mom asked if I would be there when she told the boys.

How do you prepare for moments like that? I had no idea the first time and had nothing for this round either.

We found out a dear friend in our church was diagnosed with end stage cancer out of nowhere. No indications. No *been sick for a while*. Just, boom. And he's gone in less than a year.

His daughter was a highly active leader in our group, and we were all a wreck. Oh, I forgot to mention at the end of his battle, her mom was diagnosed with breast cancer. *Hold on, Hun. I think I have a Bible verse and some wise Pastor sayings that'll really pick you up right now.*

These are just a few of 'em. But the big one, the one that almost did me in, came Father's Day of 2019.

We had just left church when my phone rang. It was a young man who had been in my ministry since the 6th grade and was now an adult leader with me.

I could barely understand him, he was so distraught. He finally calmed down enough to tell me that his best friend, another young man who had grown up in our church, had died.

There will be certain kids who just become superstars in your ministry. They have that personality and smile, and every kid loves them. They're at everything you do and even though we're not supposed to have favorites, they become one of them. That was him and suddenly he was gone.

I sat on my back porch just trembling, no words. As my heart broke for my boy who called me, I was also wrestling with my own sudden insecurities and doubts. *This was just too much. I couldn't let myself get emotionally connected to these kids like this anymore.* I thought it was over. I was done.

We had now ventured far off the path of what I had expected when I signed up for this. I felt like every time I would catch my breath from one tragedy, another would hit.

Thomas Manton said, "A soldier's strength is never known in times of peace." Well, if that was true, we were about to see what I was made of. Unfortunately, I was fairly sure it wasn't going to impress anyone.

My emotions were a wreck, my heart was heavy, and my zeal was fading fast.

God moved in me during this season and assured me that these things wouldn't break me, but I was hurting, and I was scared. Regardless, I had enlisted to fight! I was dedicated to standing on the frontlines and marching forward no matter how afraid I was.

This is where ministry can make you or break you and I wasn't about to let the enemy fly a victory flag. So, I declared, *let the battle continue!*

No one ever told me that grief felt so like fear."

– C.S. Lewis, A Grief Observed

NOTHING LEFT TO GIVE

Chapter 4
Nothing Left to Give

One thing you'll learn quickly is that this calling of ours will draw on your emotions more than almost anything else. But it's the whole reason we do what we do... because we care. It's called *compassion* and it's what makes us most like Jesus. Matthew 9:36 backs it up.

"When He saw the crowds, He had compassion on them because they were confused and helpless, like sheep without a shepherd."

Sound familiar? That's why we said *Yes* to the job offer. We care! However, compassion can reach places in your heart that you never knew existed. It can make you feel things you've never felt before. When that's new, or reaches a level you're not used to, it's intense.

The moment my first daughter was born, something inside of me changed. A place in my heart was ignited which had previously been non-existent. There was a new love and compassion that I had heard about, but I really underestimated. Others had assured me, "When you have kids of your own, you'll understand." And they were right.

It was different than how I cared about my friends, my prized possessions, and my own family. If my compassion level was at a 6 before, it was off the charts, unmeasurable at this point. For the first time, I got a small, minuscule understanding of the way God feels about us.

Then came our second daughter. Compassion overload! I had turned into a mushy, soft hearted, emotional mess, but a good mess. I hurt when they hurt. I was sad when they were sad. I celebrated when they celebrated. My heart was so tied to someone else's life, that I would never be the same.

Now, I'm not comparing the love that I have for my daughters to the kids in my church, but care and compassion had become an unmistakable factor in how I operated. And it's powerful.

If you're going into ministry for the right reasons, compassion is the fuel that fires you up. But it can also be the same fire that burns you out.

As I sat on the back porch after that Father's Day phone call, I couldn't help but start questioning my own effectiveness. Is anything I've been doing over the past two decades even working? Am I even any good at this?

I wrestled with those questions for days and just couldn't shake the feeling of defeat. I started to heal a little bit, getting my mind right again, but then came his memorial service.

It was held outdoors at a local park, and wave after wave of former students began to show up. I scanned the crowd only to see countless faces of kids who had graduated, not only from school, but seemingly from their faith.

These were kids I remember at times on their knees, weeping during worship sessions, leading their school's Christian clubs, bugging me endlessly about what other events we could do to reach their friends.

They were at every camp, every mission trip, every service, and every event. But now, it seemed their lives were headed in a different direction.

Some looked at me as if to say, "Why would that God you talked about do this?" Some didn't even acknowledge me at all. It felt like a galaxy far, far away from that first tragedy where we sat together in my little mobile home and cried together as a church family.

What happened? What happened to the influence? What happened to the passion? What happened to them and an even deeper question, what happened to *me*?

You see, in the beginning we're excited! We get a title, maybe an office that we can decorate in our home football team's merch (Go Bucs!). We get a church credit card, a key to the building, some authority, and we get to go nuts with creativity! It's a dream come true; it really is. We were gonna change the world, one teen at a time!

Now I stood there contemplating the career decision I made years ago, feeling like I wasted the church's time, the kids' time, the parent's time, my time, and worse, God's time.

Please, don't let anything I say here make you think I don't give the Lord a mental high-five because of how fortunate I am. I have one of the greatest opportunities in the world to impact lives. But at times, it just feels like I'm terrible at it.

Now, this is where others would jump in and say things like, "That's just the enemy putting those things in your head. Those kids love you. He wants you to quit because you are a threat to his plan... blah blah, blah."

But they're right. Absolutely right. I know those things aren't true. The devil is *particularly good* at kicking us while we're down. It's when we're most vulnerable. It's easier for him that way. In fact, keep in mind what it teaches us in 1 Peter 5:8 (NLT).

"Stay alert! Watch out for your great enemy, the devil. He prowls around like a roaring lion, looking for someone to devour."

What a better time than during a tragic loss, to treat you like a fawn with a broken leg trapped in some bushes?

I *know* those kids haven't forgotten how it felt to be tuned in to the Holy Spirit during one of our services or retreats.

I *know* they remember the times of being surrounded by people who cared for them and wanted to see them be what God desired.

I *know* they appreciate the times that we showed up at their house at 11pm to talk them through something or visited them in the hospital when they tried to end their own life.

I *know* they are grateful for the times that we repeatedly checked up on them after they were getting bullied in school or when their parents went through a divorce.

I *know* they felt valued when they needed to live at our house for a few days, after they got kicked out of theirs.

We didn't do those things because it made us a superstar. We did it because of, here's the magic word again, *compassion*. It's because we carry the heart and Spirit of Jesus that refuses to watch people suffer. And we want to be good at it, don't we?

It's normal to feel deflated when we encounter a loss of any kind. It's easy to be caught in the *valley of the shadow of death* and forget about the mountain top moments.

You may feel like you have nothing left but ask the Holy Spirit to remind you of the small *wins,* that far outnumber the devil's attempts to leave us broken and defeated. Let those past victories refuel you, giving you fresh wind and a full tank to keep moving you forward.

"Oh no. The Presents. They'll be destroyed... And I care! What is the DEAL?!"

- How The Grinch Stole Christmas - 2000

"Ministry Is 24 Hours"

What I Wish I Knew When I Was New

Chapter 5
Ministry is 24-Hours

This is one of the most dangerous phrases you'll hear in our field. But I want to take some pressure off you right now.

That's a lie.

I'm not saying it's completely inaccurate, there's some truth in it. But if you're going to survive in this field long-term, you'd better learn how to avoid this monster *quickly*. I heard people say it all the time when I was new and trying to network and learn. They would tell me, "Yeah, our job is never done. We're always on the clock. You gotta be ready to jump into action whenever your people need you." It wasn't long before I started repeating it myself.

I bought into it and for MANY years allowed it to set the pace for my life, for my job, and let's remember it's still a *job*.

Title it what you want: calling, mission, or whatever, my job became the front and center of everything. I talked about it at dinner, while watching TV, or lying-in bed.

Family trips to Disney or restaurants became some kind of "inspiration" that I needed to write down immediately. How they greeted people, designed a room, the ambiance - everything became *research*. While my wife was taking pictures of our kids with

Mickey and Minnie, I was taking pictures of how they had their lighting rig setup. My work/life balance was pretty, well... unbalanced.

I remember the first time Nicholle called me out on it. Our kids were at karate class, and I was working on Sunday lessons while we sat there. I missed something cool that one of our kids did and she said, "I remember you used to talk smack about Dads who missed their kids' things because of their jobs. Now you're doing the same thing."

Dang.

I'd like to say that was the turning point, but I just continued to do the same things. I fooled myself into thinking, *if I just talked about work stuff*, it was different. But it wasn't. It's all that came out of my mouth. It's all that filled my thoughts. Afterall, I had a very important job with souls on the line and I had to pour everything I had into it, and people needed to understand that.

If I took a day off, I would feel guilty. If I stopped thinking of new ways to reach more kids, I felt like I was slacking.

I don't speak for everyone here, but we seem to think bragging about long hours and talking about how *ministry never takes time off* is some kind of indication of our importance or makes us sound impressive.

Comments are made, "He's so dedicated to those kids. He just never stops." And we bask in it. We LOVE it. That's pride, folks. If we're not careful, it almost becomes a "savior" mentality.

For me, it wasn't uncommon to answer every phone call on the first ring. It wasn't uncommon to run out because some kid broke up with his girlfriend after four months and needed to talk because he was *sad*. It wasn't uncommon to "shush" my kids when I was on the phone or hurry my wife through her story to tell her what little TJ did during a small group. It wasn't uncommon to be clueless.

Here's a story that kicks me in the throat every time I recall it. I had a makeshift office set up at home with a dry-erase calendar. Lemme tell ya, when I hung up that calendar and added stuff to it, I felt super legit. I had never had a job where I had to track things like that.

One day my oldest daughter casually came in to talk to me and looked at it. Amidst the meetings and deadlines written on it was a school concert in which she was performing. She looked at it, with no sarcasm or ill-will, just the innocent remark of a child and said, "Wow, you put me on your calendar!" Then she turned and walked away.

Come on! For real? Talk about a wakeup call. From that point on, the first thing I write on any calendar, even to this day, is family stuff and it's always in red. Nothing else gets red! Meetings? Blue. Events?

Green. Red is reserved to remind me of humility and priority. Hey, if the "red letters" are important enough for the words of Jesus, they're important enough for my family.

The Fishbowl

While we're on the topic of family, let's get real about something I learned rather quickly. It fits with the idea of always being *on*. You may not be married or have kids, but this can even apply to you alone. Our family used to refer to it as *the fishbowl*.

Imagine you go to an aquarium or have a fish tank at home. What's the goal? Watch the fish, duh! The glass allows you to observe these amazing creatures in their man-made, faux, natural habitat. You get to see how they interact with the others and how they act at feeding time.

Now, not to be gross here, but you've probably seen a fish... well... poop in the water. Or maybe you've watched another fish attacking one of its tank-mates. If they do anything unusual or unexpected, we gasp or giggle and tell everyone around us to pay attention. Then we roll video and post it on social media to share our unbelief. Often, we're so captivated that we just want to stand there and watch for the next incident. I mean, that's the concept of the glass enclosure anyway, right? Observation.

In ministry, as unfair as it can be at times, we live in

a fishbowl. Everybody's observing you, and your family. It reminds me of *Roz* from Monster's Inc. "I'm watching you, Wazowski. Always watching."

I fully understand what it says in 1 Timothy 3 about the lifestyle and expectations of church leaders, how they are held to an extremely high standard. And yes, we should be. But if we're honest, as a follower of Jesus, shouldn't these be the standards we *all* have to live by? The short answer to that is *yes*, but that's another book for another time.

My point is the people who are watching you and your family can unfortunately be just like the people observing the fishbowl. They're often waiting to see something gasp worthy and gossip-ready to jump on. They forget that *you* are the one in the leadership spotlight and think your family should be held to their *holier than thou* standards too. That's incredibly unfair.

As your kids are trying to tread water through their adolescent years and figure life out, God forbid they wear something, say something, or post something that doesn't meet the church-approved checklist.

God forbid, your spouse doesn't attend every church bake sale. God forbid, they post a picture on vacation of them in a bathing suit or with a glass of wine. This may seem like an extreme example… it's not. It may not be the case for some church environments, but it is for many.

I'm fine with the shots I've taken over the years because I know you won't please everyone. I've matured enough to be able to take it and respond appropriately, taking cues from *James 1:19 (NIV)*

"My dear brothers and sisters, take note of this: Everyone should be quick to listen, slow to speak and slow to become angry...."

However, my wife doesn't deserve it, my kids don't deserve it, and I must always do my best to protect them. Are they perfect? No. But neither are their critics, yet the gawkers will gawk. Stand guard for them.

Thanks for letting me get a little sidetracked there. I just felt that was important to mention.

The Office

When I went full-time in 2003, we didn't have offices, since we met in a rented movie theater. We all just worked from home, which seemed dreamy.

If you've ever worked from home you know, working from home isn't all it's cracked up to be. My home was my job, and my job was my home. There was no distinction between the two. This meant it was much harder for me to shut down. "Work" was too convenient, but it helped me get a ton done... all the time.

Let's go back to that word *convenient* though. I don't

think I have to break this down for you. There's a lot of ways that convenience can be your enemy.

A couple of years ago, after building our facilities, our Senior Pastor sent the staff an awful, rude, demanding, heartless email that read, "Starting in January we will begin working from the offices on campus."

What? Are you kidding me? What a disruption to my life. I had been accustomed to working this way for years and now, he had the nerve to ask us to work from the office.

Now I was gonna spend more money on gas, not to mention the wear and tear on my car and be captive to a set schedule. I'm being dramatic here of course. None of us felt that way, but it was definitely a shift. Little did I know, it was one of the greatest things I had ever been instructed to do.

After settling into my new workspace, I found something interesting had happened. I had developed *work hours*. This was new to me.

God began to show me that it was ok to *clock out*. If I didn't get something finished, I could pick it back up the next day when I came back in. Plus, I didn't realize how distracted I had been at home.

Sure, I had gotten a lot done there and learned to be productive with a good deal of self-discipline, but not like I thought. I began to see how easy it had been to think, *I really need to vacuum. I should do that real fast,* or *I gotta get those dishes done and the dogs walked,* and so on, and so on. Sometimes I would put on the news and catch myself staring over my computer screen to catch the weather forecast (in Florida summers, that's really important) only to ignore my work project for a half hour or so.

With my new office routine, I found something that was refreshing; I would shut my computer down, pack up, and actually leave. Leaving meant the workday was done. Period.

It was mentally refreshing, physically refreshing, and even spiritually refreshing. I could decompress on the way home and give my family all of me, my undivided attention. Don't misunderstand me, there will be times where you must run out or do something. There will be times where people will need your presence or attention. But that's where good discernment comes in.

I discovered an amazing invention during that time… voicemail! When my phone rang, I no longer answered it at lightning speed, I didn't drop my dinner fork to save the distressed individual on the other line. I learned to screen calls.

These days we're lucky enough to get a text instead of a call which makes it easier to respond to when it's convenient, but in my early years it was an actual call. I learned to let it go to voicemail. I'll check it when I get a chance and respond accordingly.

If Matt wants to know if I'll paint a skull on his guitar, we can talk tomorrow.

If Marsean got a flat tire and is stuck on the side of the road with no spare or AAA, I'm on it.

If Michael wants to know my view on the book of Revelation, well, he'll have to find someone who actually understands it, but we'll catch up later.

Here's some validation you really need to hear. Ready?

It's ok to turn it off, in fact it's vital.

People want immediate access to you; in fact, some believe it's required of you. After all, they *pay your salary* with their tithes, right?

I said this earlier and maybe it'll rub some people the wrong way, but sometimes we must think of it as a *job* and not a *calling*. Clock out!

Even Jesus had to clock out sometimes. You've read these before.

Mark 6:30-32 (NLT) *"The apostles returned to Jesus from their ministry tour and told him all they had done and taught. 31 Then Jesus said, "Let's go off by ourselves to a quiet place and rest awhile." He said this because there were so many people coming and going that Jesus and his apostles didn't even have time to eat."*

Matthew 14:13 (NIV) "When Jesus heard what had happened, he withdrew by boat privately to a solitary place."

Let me help you eliminate the guilt before you even feel it - clocking out doesn't mean you don't care. In fact, it shows how much you do.

How you prioritize your time, and your own mental health, will either make you or break you. Choose wisely. The people around will benefit from it and so will you. I promise.

Chapter 6

Time Is On Our Side

Chapter 6
Time Is On Our Side

The legendary Mick Jagger once sang, "Time is on my side." Some of you just sang it in your head, some of you are too young to know who I'm talking about. The Rolling Stones, Mick Jagger, look it up.

Lots of people would disagree with his philosophy and see time as a stressor and a nemesis. Think about how many times you've heard someone say, "If only there were more hours in a day," or something similar. We are bound to the clock for most of our lives.

True story, when my wife's uncle would go on vacation, he would literally leave his watch at home. He refused to be a slave to the clock. Genius. While no one can actually give you more time, there's a way to make you feel like there's more available time, and help you make the most of every minute.

I don't claim to be *great* at many things, or ANY thing actually; but for some reason, time management is a super-power of mine. Without trying, I just discovered that I have a unique ability to get tons of stuff done in small amounts of time.

This isn't one of those, *I work better under pressure* things. It's a *work better so I don't have pressure* thing. I just easily find *the zone*. Besides, I've never been a procrastinator, at least as an adult.

I hate the feeling of being crushed by the clock. My inner voice always says things like, *What if something goes wrong? What if there's an emergency and now you can't meet the deadline?*

I'm a *pretty mellow* dude, so feeling rushed and stressed because I didn't use my time wisely just seems, well, dumb. Why would I want to put myself through that if all I had to do was use some wisdom?

Let me share four of the Principles I use that keep me productive and allow me to keep pace with the clock - and maybe even free up some time for the golf range.

1. Do it Now!

This one seems simple, but for some people it's really a struggle. When you make it a habit, whether at work or everyday life, even in small things, it's a beauty. You get an email that needs a response; do it now (but not if you're clocked out and it can wait until tomorrow). Something laying on your desk needs to be put away; do it now. You see the floor needs swept; do it now. You get the idea.

So often, we fall victim to *procrastination*, even if we're not a procrastinator, but it actually works against the clock and your schedule. All we're really doing is building a pile of stress we have to deal with eventually. I don't know why we do this to ourselves. It's so counterproductive and such a bad habit to let develop.

And it's little stuff. For example, someone will text us, and they just need a simple answer. But we ignore it, until they embarrassingly remind us. To get my attention, my daughters will emphasize their text with a little question mark on it.

Here's an example where my superpowers don't kick in. My wife will do laundry, put all my shirts on a hanger, and lay them at the end of the bed. Instead of hanging them up at bedtime, I move them to the floor because *I'm too tired to put them away*. By the end of the week, she's added to the pile and now I'm thinking of how I may pass out from exhaustion, having to put them all away at once. Even if it's the unimportant things, just do it now!

2. What can I do while I'm waiting?

This concept is my golden nugget! I *love* this one. My previous job required me to occasionally work in filing. We would scan barcodes, check some info, and then slap a label on the folder for it to be filed away. It was terrible. Super monotonous, super boring. I hated it when I saw that I was scheduled to be there. The mandatory speed was 35 folders per hour.

Well, my super-power kicked in one day and I discovered a few things I could do while waiting for the computer to do its thing. I had free time and a free hand so why waste either?

I began to prepare the next folder on the unused side

of my desk. When the label finally spit out the previous one, BOOM! I was already a minute or so ahead of schedule. This concept catapulted me into the most hated guy in filing because I began cranking out 75 per hour!

Managers loved me and co-workers despised me as I became the new *trainer* and minimum requirements went up.

I use this concept, literally, every single day, in so many ways, almost unconsciously at this point.

As I wait for the rice to cook, I unload and load the dishwasher instead of playing on my phone.

As I sit in the car repair shop, I work on sermons or blogs instead of playing on my phone.

Just last night, while I was cooking on the grill outside, I put in two plants that needed replacing instead of... you're way ahead of me, I'm sure.

What can I do while I'm waiting? Ask yourself that question every time you find yourself in a holding pattern. You'll be shocked how much you get done, and how much you get ahead.

3. Eat the frog!

I learned this one from a Pastor named Nelson Searcy. I'm not sure if it's his original idea, but it's phenomenal and has changed how I think. It's similar to the first one, but different in its context.

Imagine you have a desk full of things to do and one of them is to eat a live frog. Nothing in you wants to do it (I hope) but it *must* be done. So, you put it off; over and over and over, doing other stuff first.

The problem is it never goes away. He sits there and you see him out of the corner of your eye, knowing what's inevitable. His croaking becomes distracting and it's hard to focus on the task at hand.

We all have that *frog*. The phone call you dread making, the email you don't wanna respond to, the mandatory thing you hate to do most. It sits there and nags at us and in turn, makes us *less* productive, because it steals our thoughts and motivation.

Here's a weird, but effective way I have used this principle in my own life. Our old house sat on a little over an acre of land, so I used a riding lawn mower. The septic tank and its pipes coming from the side of the house made it really challenging to mow around. I would have to stop, turn off the blades, back up, move over, re-engage the blade, cut a strip, stop, turn off the blades, rinse and repeat like 8 times.

Typical for Florida, our dirt was a bit sandy; so, the dirt, sand, and grass would shoot out against the house and fly back on me. By the time I was done mowing, I was filthy and had 6 gallons of dirt in my eyes, mouth, and hair. I used to leave it to the end, hoping it would maybe start raining so I wouldn't have to finish it. Not smart or productive.

When I learned *the frog* concept, you can imagine what I started to do. Yep! I fired up the mower and went right for it. Once it was done, I felt so relieved. Then I knew I had a smooth, flat, clean ride in front of me. Sure, I was covered in dirt, but at least it was over.

Eat the frog! Do it first, get it done, and move on to the things you would rather be doing, with full focus. Time is a gift from God. It's a gift we are expected to be good stewards of. Trying to squeeze in family, work, ministry, and anything in between is tough. I get that. But I honestly believe if you walk in wisdom and become less distracted, you'll breathe easier and just maybe, have some time for yourself.

4. PLAN AHEAD!

This is maybe the hardest for some people, but it's amazingly liberating when done right. Get yourself a planner and plan! Plan your message series for the whole quarter (yes, you can change a week or two if the Spirit leads that way).

If possible, write as many sermons in one week as you can. If you have a week off for a guest speaker or special event, write your next sermon that week anyway. Then you free yourself up to maybe add some creative elements or work on something else *or* give yourself a free day!

Plan out your upcoming meeting agendas, start planning pieces of your summer camp even if it's eight months away. Plan for Christmas, Easter, or other big events way ahead of time. When you plan and prepare like that, it takes the pressure off getting everything done at the last minute which, as we all know, makes the seconds click off a little faster (not literally but it feels that way). *Pay now, play later* as they say.

These four principles have impacted my productivity and my stress level in great ways. I still don't go to the golf range, which is evident if you ever saw me play. But I can take a nap if I ever need to, and I won't feel guilty!

Time really is on your side if you manage it well.

Ephesians 5:15-17 "Look carefully then how you walk, not as unwise but as wise, making the best use of the time, because the days are evil. Therefore, do not be foolish, but understand what the will of the Lord is."

What I Wish I Knew When I Was New

Chapter 7

Build Your Team

What I Wish I Knew When I Was New

Chapter 7
Build Your Team

When I first started out, it was me and eight kids. No band, no media team, no small group leaders, no anything. It was easy for me to cover all the roles needed because, well, there weren't any at the time.

We would do worship time with the adults in the movie theater we were renting, and then I would lead them to another theater where I led the rip-and-read lesson plan each week. That was pretty much it. It wasn't that difficult. If we took a field trip, I did the promotion, I did sign ups, I drove the van, I made sure everyone got home.

As the group began to grow, we started adding some new elements to our ministry. We started a worship team, added media slides, sound, and then eventually a small group study. The problem was I couldn't do it all anymore.

I was trying to lead the worship team, create logos or graphics for flyers (yeah actual paper flyers), keep the attention of a new small group Bible study group (which was growing beyond what would be a *small group*), among a handful of other jobs. It was like one of my favorite Bugs Bunny scenes, if you're old enough to remember it.

Bugs is on a baseball team and he's the only player. The announcer goes through the lineup saying

"Pitching - Bugs Bunny, First base - Bugs Bunny, Second base - Bugs Bunny, Shortstop - Daffy Duck." Just kidding, it was Bugs again.

I tried my best to run everything as long as I could, but that didn't last long. I had to find help. I had to build a team that could help me expand our ministry and share some of the responsibilities.

Can I be honest though? This was hard at first. Not because I couldn't find people, although that was part of it, but because of, dare I say, *pride*.

I had gotten rather good at covering all the bases and it's the first time I'd been *The Guy*. I'm not proud of it, but that's the truth. Word of advice: if you're currently *The Guy* or *The Gal*... you're not Bugs Bunny. You'll lose the game if you don't allow other people to use their God-given gifts and play too.

Baseball teams have hitting coaches, pitching coaches, first and third base coaches, etc., for a reason. The head coach can't give 100% to every person on the team, nor do they have the knowledge of every position.

If someone wants to join your team who is an advanced audio technician, skilled musician, finance guru, insane event planner, LET 'EM PLAY! This will only advance your chances of creating a program that succeeds, and isn't that what you want? I hope so.

Here's some stuff I learned, sometimes the hard way.

1. You need leaders of the opposite sex

If you're a male leader, there are things a young lady needs help with, and you have nothing to offer, and vice-versa.

I recall my daughter, 13 at the time, was having a difficult day and we were arguing over something or another. She said, "You just don't understand."

I replied, "You're right! I've never been a 13-year-old girl before!" Thankfully, we had some great female leaders on our team (as well as her rockstar Mom) that she could lean into when needed.

You need to cover both sides with leaders who understand their crowd and can offer appropriate and helpful advice. Also, it's a great safety protocol. Mixing genders is fine for your big group stuff, but not when it comes down to the real life, mentoring relationships that these young people need.

2. You need QUALIFIED leaders

Ugh. This pains me to even write it. When you're new and eager to build a team, you'll take anyone crazy enough to want to work with teenagers. The minute a warm-bodied human walks up, smiles, and says, "I'd love to help in your youth ministry," we're so excited that we throw them a t-shirt and a lanyard. We don't even consider that this may be a ticking time-bomb.

I've had my fair share of volunteers who, God bless em,' had good intentions, but they ended up being terrible with kids. They had no patience, struggled to show grace, and forgot that the world of teens looks a lot different than when they were a kid, 20 or 30 years ago. When that happens, it's really easy for that volunteer to begin pulling your ministry in a different direction to meet their own agendas or simply just fail to connect and minister to our crowd.

I'm not saying every volunteer needs to be a scholar, theologian, counselor, or Mother Teresa. We all have space to grow. But as Bill Hybels wrote in his amazingly helpful book *Axioms*, you *gotta* have the "right people on the bus."

Interview, get references, get to know them so that they can serve well and serve kids well. It'll save you the anxiety of knowing you have to *fire* a volunteer. Trust me on this one.

3. Don't be afraid to let youth serve

Actually, be afraid, but don't be reluctant. We've found that our *most* successful volunteers and also our *least* successful volunteers, have been kids. That's a helpful statement, right?

My point is, give them a chance. Letting kids serve in their own ministry gives them ownership and belonging. They take more pride in your ministry when they see God using their gifting. It gives them confidence and teaches them responsibility.

We've always used youth to help with AV stuff, be on the worship team, greet, etc. Think about it, most of them know more about tech stuff than we do anyway, so take advantage of that.

Last year we allowed one of our high school girls to take over our social media. She's *way* more in touch with what will attract her friends and peers than any of us adults are. It's a *win-win* and you want as many *wins* as possible.

"But Earl, you said they're also your LEAST successful volunteers?" Yep, that's true too.

We've had kids join the worship team only to not show up or even quit a couple of months after. It's common for the kid running lights or sound to be a no-show or *call out* because he and his friends were up too late playing Fortnite.

Here's a couple of things to note:

> #1 - It's important to have depth, just like a sports team. We need a couple of people who can serve the same role. We often train kids to learn multiple roles in case we need someone to come off the bench on any given day.
>
> It's also a good idea to always have an adult

trained in these areas as well, especially if they are super dependable.

#2 - Remember they're kids. They're not full-time paid staff. They can be inconsistent, undependable, and frustrating. But again, they're kids. Think about how dedicated and motivated you were at that age.

Don't put them in charge of an area, don't make them the CEO of the media team. Just give them a chance and work around their potential inconsistencies. It's still worth it to show them that they can be a part of what God is doing in your church.

#3 - Think ahead. I try to cut down on inconsistency issues by sending out schedules. Ask them, or better yet, their parents, what weekends they are not available.

We have a couple of kids on our serving teams who play competitive sports. This means there's a good chance they won't be there on multiple Sundays within a season.

Once I know everyone's availability, I make the schedule and send it to them, but... also send it to the parents! They are the real calendar keepers and Uber drivers to everything their kids are involved in. Keep them in the loop and it'll save you a headache or two.

4. Train them

I know it seems obvious, but it's so important. Now when I say *training*, I don't mean, *This is the sound board. Just make sure it all sounds good.* Explain highs, lows, feedback, reverb, balance, etc.

Train your small group leaders on things like *why* we don't have closed-door one-on-one meetings with kids or how to deal with disruptive youth, rather than *Here's your lesson guide. Good luck in there.*

In our church, we create job description sheets that every volunteer gets so they're really clear on expectations, qualifications, and details of their role. I know this takes time, but I promise you that the time invested is well spent. It'll actually save you time by not having to course-correct volunteers who are unsure of how to fulfill their roles.

It also builds confidence in your volunteers. Think about how you perform a task when you are well-informed about it, as opposed to when it's brand new.

Lastly, it shows your volunteers that you take what you do seriously. Your level of training sets the bar for your expectations of the performance.

5. Love on your team

Pretty much all of your adult volunteers will have full time jobs, and/or have kids. They have bills to pay, soccer practices to be on time for, a household to run, etc. They have a full plate. As for your youth volunteers, they have homework, dance class, chores, and maybe even a job depending on how old they are. My point is, your volunteers have lives, real lives, real busy lives! Anything they are doing for you is out of their heart to serve God and serve the church. ALWAYS remind them that you know and respect that.

When we do our pre-service Huddle Time (a time for our team to go over the plan for the day and cover details) I always start out with, "Thank you all so much for doing this. I'd be lost without you," or some version of that.

If you have it on your budget, every so often get them a little gift card for the local ice cream or coffee shop. It doesn't have to be big or expensive, just heartfelt. "Thank you" notes are really cheap, but everyone knows that a handwritten note is just special. Find ways to make sure they know how much you appreciate them. Care for them and they'll care for your students in the same way.

Again, from the very beginning, build your team! You can't do it alone, nor should you want to.

I'd recommend picking up the book *No More Lone Rangers: How to Build a Team-Centered Youth Ministry* by David Chow. He goes into much more detail, and it really helped me a ton when it was time for this next step.

"Alone, we can only move buckets. But if we work together, we can drain rivers."

Mike Brady - The Brady Bunch Movie

What I Wish I Knew When I Was New

A Little Help Here, Please

What I Wish I Knew When I Was New

Chapter 8
A Little Help Here, Please

In passing, I previously mentioned something that I called *rip and read* lessons and I want to dive into that a little more. These things saved my life in the first couple of years.

They were a collection of workbooks called *Talksheets* by David Lynn. You can actually still get them on christianbook.com and other websites. They may even have a digital version by now.

These things were awesome (expect when you're working on them during your kids' karate class). They had nearly 50 lessons to choose from and some could fit together as a series. They gave you the Bible verse, complete with background and context, and then it would lay out discussion questions.

Even a guy like me, with no Bible knowledge whatsoever, could facilitate a great meeting if you prepared well enough in advance. I would make enough copies for the whole group (about 8 of them), hand them out, and we would actually have some really great study time.

After a couple of years using those, I felt like I was ready to begin writing my own sermons. They weren't fancy. In fact, I would dare to say they weren't any good. If you could talk to those kids, they would probably agree. But I got better over time.

I figured out that a couple of my spiritual gifts were teaching and communicating; and I've always loved being creative, so writing messages and creating a Sunday morning program was becoming really fun. I found ways to use my sense of humor and creativity to craft lessons that seemed to stick pretty well with the crowd. I was getting good feedback from the kids and my team, so the *Talksheets* era ended. Years went by and 100's of sermons were written.

The freedom-of-creativity element was the best! I was preaching from canoes on stage, riding motorcycles into the room, firing up weed-eaters and lawnmowers (word of advice, make sure to open the windows if you do that one). Chainsaws through watermelons, preaching from the roof outside, bashing a piñata (another piece of advice, make sure it's not in swinging distance of a hanging fluorescent light). All of this in order to get the message of Jesus out in ways that kids could relate to and remember. And it was working really well. I felt like a REAL Pastor.

And then our Children's Pastor, the Pastor's wife, brought up the "C" word.

The "C" word

Hettie, my coworker, but more importantly a great friend, had begun to use a new... here it is... *Curriculum*. It was from an organization called *Orange*, which had introduced a youth ministry version and she suggested that I take a look.

* Disclaimer - This is not an attempt to promote Orange. I don't work for them. My Uncle doesn't run it. I have no ties to them. They don't pay me. But they really are amazing.

I told her I would check it out, so I did. And she was right, it was great, as expected. But there were two problems:

1. It was costly (until you break down what you actually get).

2. I was already writing my own stuff. I felt like I didn't need help.

Our church was willing to pay for the subscription, so that wasn't the issue. The issue was me and my pride. I felt like it meant, I was not a REAL Pastor if I was just using someone else's work. I believed that I had to be original in order to be legit.

But I went back and took another look at it with more of an open mind. They offered things I had no time to do. Things that would enhance our ministry in great ways, like full series layouts for the entire year, small group discussions, series graphics, and message intro videos. They included prewritten resources to send to parents, stage design ideas, worship leader guides, games, social media guides, and so much more.

Now, was I capable of doing most of these things on my own? Sure. But for the whole year at one time? Nope. At a professional level like they offered... No way.

This was like my *Talksheets,* but on steroids! By swallowing my pride and trying it, I was able to take our program to new levels.

I could spend more time caring for my team members, and I was able to concentrate more on some of the things that were getting glanced over, while I tried to get messages and studies written every week.

But wait, what about the canoes, chainsaws, motorcycles, and carbon monoxide poisoning lawnmower creativity? Was I really willing to give that up by using someone else's material? Have I now become un-legit (not sure that's a real word)?

Don't reinvent the wheel, just decorate the spokes

The numbers differ slightly depending on what information you read, but it's believed the wheel was invented by Ancient Mesopotamian people, sometime between 4200-4000 BC. It was most likely originally used in creating pottery and then later adapted for farming equipment, transportation, and then rollerblades.

Here's the crazy thing. If you were to look at a wheel 5000+ years ago and a wheel now... pretty consistent! Not much has changed. One shape worked then, and the same shape works now. Nothing needs to be added to a circle to make it roll better.

In boxing, there's really just four main punches: the jab, the cross, the hook, and the uppercut. That's it. There's nothing really fancy about it. Great boxers have learned to create variations and combinations of those four moves that help them outwit their opponent.

Record-breaking Olympic swimmers have four main strokes: the Butterfly, the Backstroke, the Breaststroke, and Freestyle. Occasionally they will have a *Medley*, which is a combination of all four strokes in various parts of a single race. Swimmers can make slight adjustments in their hands, feet, and even in their breathing to gain that extra half a second.

In bowling, (my sport of choice) you have a sixty foot lane, ten pins, and a ball to knock them down with. You still get 10 frames to get your best score. Bowlers can choose from different kinds of bowling balls to help manipulate the oil pattern put on the lane, but... the ball is still round.

A car has always had four wheels, a motor, and a steering wheel. Now, cars have obviously come a long way since the Model T, with powered accessories, cigarette lighters, and things to create a more comfortable ride. But, overall, it's still four wheels, a motor, and a steering wheel.

There are some things that just don't need a lot of changing. They work just fine, but sometimes a little innovation can be magic.

Let's talk about the word "Innovate" for a second. The Webster definition is - *to make changes in something established, especially by introducing new methods, ideas, or products.*

Innovation takes something that already exists and adapts it, changes it to work better.

Where am I going with all of this? You don't have to invent anything! In fact, in Ecclesiastes Chapter 1, verse 9 and 10, it gives us a little reassurance when it says:

"History merely repeats itself. It has all been done before. Nothing under the sun is truly new. Sometimes people say, Here is something new!" But actually, it is old; nothing is ever truly new."

You don't have to stay up all night trying to figure out the next groundbreaking ministry discovery. People have already paved the way for us. We can just innovate. This revelation took so much pressure off of me!

For me, I started off well by using *Talksheets* and the brainpower of someone who already did most of the heavy work for me. But that's also when I was just part-time with the church. I NEEDED help since I was limited on time, and also brand new.

But, once I went full-time, I had extra hours to start writing my own material and getting creative. That's when I fell into the trap of believing the extra time was supposed to be for creating 100% original content. I was trying to write my own messages, write my own Bible Studies, come up with some kind of game, make videos for message intros or special occasions.

As I grew as a leader, I started learning that my team needed more of my attention and care. I had to focus more on helping my volunteers grow and feel qualified for what we were asking them to do. It was hard to fit that in with the time I was dedicating to being *original*.

Don't reinvent the wheel, just decorate the spokes. It's okay to take the basic ideas and put some twists on them. That's how everything in history has progressed if you think about it. In the same way that boxers, swimmers, bowlers, and cars have stuck to the basics but *decorated the spokes*, we can do the same in our ministry leadership.

There should be absolutely ZERO shame in benefiting from the hard work of others, to help us serve the Lord and His people better.

I've also learned that just because I went back to using a curriculum, it doesn't mean you can't tweak things, in fact you should. I don't use it word for word or use every idea. I craft it for my own group and how we do things, so that it still has my own voice and personality.

Every youth ministry looks different. Make it fit for your crowd. You'll know what works best for your kids, and what gets their attention. Just because it's not *yours* doesn't mean you can't still make it *yours*.

There's still room for a chainsaw through a watermelon if you think hard enough. Plus, you'll get to focus on the other things that need your attention just as much as sermon prep.

Being okay with not being 100% original doesn't make you lazy or unqualified. It makes you smart!

Asking for help isn't weak, it's a great example of how to take care of yourself." – Charlie Brown

Resources

Here's a list of places some of my ministry friends use, to find GREAT stuff.

- ThinkOrange.com
- DownloadYouthMinistry.com
- Youthministry360.com
- Gamesforyouthministry.com
- thesource4ym.com
- group.com
- daretoshare.org
- growcurriculum.org

Chapter 9

This Ain't Your Turf, Man

Chapter 9
This Ain't Your Turf, Man

Early in my youth ministry career, I learned something bizarre. I tried to connect with respected youth leaders in my area, in hopes of gaining a little help from their years of wisdom. They came from large churches and had successful youth ministry backgrounds.

I had hoped they might take this new guy under their wing, to help expand some influence in our large community of lost teens. Instead, what I learned was that they were like football coaches. They had their successful ministry playbook and did their best to keep it private.

No follow up emails or phone calls, no follow through on their *Yeah man, let's get together,* after bumping into them unexpectedly. It seemed, this was their home field, and they weren't about to let some small-time coach come in and make their fans switch jerseys.

Maybe, this isn't true in your arena or even how *you* think, but I can bet someone reading this is saying, "Yep, I get it." You're looked at as *competition*, the other team, the rival church down the street, even if you're a small one. I understand how we could all think that way sometimes, but it's just... stupid.

I was left on my own, to read random books that no

one suggested, go to conferences only to be overwhelmed by all the information, and pray that I would figure this stuff out before the kids realized I had no idea what I was doing. Actually, kids are smart, and it was pretty evident I was clueless, but luckily most stuck around anyway.

My Senior Pastor has always been amazingly supportive, but he didn't do youth ministry. He didn't know the big-name people I should really be learning from, or what youth-based books I should find. It just wasn't his world. I was pretty much on my own and it was hard. And it was frustrating.

Remember, I had zero church background as a kid. I didn't grow up in a youth group, never went on a mission trip, never memorized a Bible verse, or even owned a Bible.

This youth ministry thing was about as unfamiliar and intimidating as anything in my life. I was being entrusted to inspire and lead kids into a growing relationship with Jesus, but I had only learned His story a couple of years prior. I needed someone to walk this out with me, tell me what they're reading and learning. Someone, anyone, help me!

But not in our area, oh no! These guys weren't about to spill all their hard-earned knowledge with some new guy who wants to steal their sheep.

As our ministry and my experience has grown, I try my best to not fall into this trap and make it a point to connect with others as best as possible. If I have something to offer someone who's new in the game, how ignorant and unlike Christ is it, to believe it should be *classified* information?

If we can be honest, when we refuse to help or mentor someone with the same goal as us, aren't we really hoping they fail? Let that sink in for a minute.

Aren't we secretly hoping they won't figure out the magic formula to hitting max capacity in their youth room before you do? I mean, *we* had to struggle to learn all of this, so why should we make it easy on them? Let *them* put in the mental work too. If you want it, you gotta work for it, right? No, not right at all.

I remember the first time I invited a youth pastor, who was new to our area, to breakfast. He was freshly married and new to full-time ministry. We talked about our *home field*, I shared some things I had experienced and invited him to meet the one other leader willing to hang out with me.

I wasn't worried about him taking my kids, being better than me, having a cooler facility. I love this because if we do it, we all win. He wins, I win, the community wins, the church wins, GOD wins! We can all benefit.

Here's a few reasons why networking with our peers is so important.

1. Venting!

Ricky was running a youth ministry not far from us and he was doing it well. He was younger than me, cooler than me and super smart. He was part of a coaching and leadership group and was learning so much more than I was at the time.

We somehow connected and we agreed to meet at the local Panera. I wasn't a fan of the place, but hey, I needed some help, and he was paying.

Over time, we built a bond that has lasted for years. One of the best things about our friendship was that we both had a safe place to share things we could never share with other people. It was a safe place to unload our frustrations, sufferings, and doubts.

Consider it counseling without having to lay on a couch. And honestly, who can understand you better than someone who is fighting the same battle? You'd be shocked how much turmoil your *rival team* has in common with you and how much better you feel when you leave.

You might even feel better just hearing how messed up *they* are! (Kidding... maybe) It's great to have someone to vent to, plus it's free, unless you pick up the check.

2. A community playbook

It took me a while to adjust to it, but when Ricky and I started to share playbooks, it was amazing. We've shared message ideas, stage design ideas, volunteer training ideas.

We've partnered up in speaking at local public school *Christian clubs* and would loan each other equipment if we had extra. I even called on him to help me plan our first winter retreat, since he had lots of experience and is a lot smarter than I am.

At one point we were even working on an idea to join our ministry teams to host a local youth conference. It never panned out, but it was exciting to talk about.

Imagine what an impact we could have if we were willing to make our successful plays public. I know Tom Brady would never email his offensive strategies to his opponent, but we're not out to win a Super Bowl. We're out to win souls and we could all use a good trick play, to keep the devil a step behind.

3. Power in numbers

Ricky and I live in the same neighborhood and our kids go to the same schools. Honestly, why shouldn't we work together to build a mega-team of soul-winners? I mean, we both have the same Kingdom-minded goal, which is to mobilize our kids to make Jesus-powered change in their community.

I always think of the scene in the movie *A Bug's Life*, where the ants realize how powerful they can be if they join forces against the enemy Hopper. That scene of them lining up behind each other and linking arms is such a powerful picture of what we could do together. Same for us. It's not *my* church, *their* church, *this* church, *that* church, but *the* church!

I think youth leaders ministering to the same areas should remember this truth.

Ecclesiastes 4:12 "A person standing alone can be attacked and defeated, but two can stand back-to-back and conquer. Three are even better, for a triple-braided cord is not easily broken."

Maybe, it's time we stopped trying to win the attendance Super Bowl and polishing our trophies for being the powerhouse district youth ministry.

Maybe, we should swallow some pride, come together, and open our playbooks with each other.

Maybe, you need to reach out to someone who can help you or maybe, reach out to someone who *you* can help.

You may be surprised at how many battles we begin winning, with more coaches on the same team.

"The man who can keep a secret may be wise, but he is not half as wise as the man with no secrets to keep." –Edgar Watson Howe

Chapter 10

Oil Check

What I Wish I Knew When I Was New

Chapter 10
Oil Check

Several years ago, I found myself sitting in a secluded cabin in the woods of Tennessee. When I say secluded, I mean we feared slightly for our lives as we drove up the side of a mountain to find the place.

The dirt road leading to the cabin looked like it was built more as a one-way path for a motorcycle, than for two cars heading in opposite directions. If this trip was meant to relax, it wasn't starting off well. But we survived and vacation had begun.

I went to the cabin with only a few expectations:

- Experience a real vacation outside of Florida. Disney's great, but I needed more.
- Relax.
- Hear God, clearly and intensely.

We weren't there for the attractions and tourist traps. We didn't make a schedule and plan things down to the hour. We just wanted peace and quiet, and to escape the busyness of what we all experience most days.

Can I be a bit transparent and honest with you guys though? Can I drop the *Painless Pastor* stuff for a few minutes and spill my guts?

Before we left, I was feeling a bit *sluggish*. I could

feel myself slowing down. My drive for ministry was sluggish, my motivation to plan was sluggish, and my creativity was sluggish. The scariest thing is that my passion to move forward was sluggish.

The last quarter of the ministry year was wearing on me, but not because things were *bad*, it was just... a lot. We had begun planning for a new youth building, planning for the next year, seeing attendance goals for the current year slip out of our reach, and watching people's lives disintegrate, despite the advice I had poured out.

If you're a Pastor (or in ministry at all), you know the deal. I'm not saying anything you don't get and I'm not saying my struggle is something unique. I just think that after years of very minimal soul maintenance, it had caught up.

The T-Bird

Many years ago, my wife and I bought a super kick-butt Ford Thunderbird. This thing was awesome. Quick, sleek, comfortable seats and even a cool keypad on the door, where you type a code in, to lock and unlock it. For us, that was high-class. This was nothing like we had ever owned. Now if you're a car person, I want to warn you about what you're about to read. It's disturbing and painful. You've been warned.

I put over 70,000 miles on the T-Bird, and never changed the oil. I was immature when it came to maintenance. I just never thought about it. Until that day... that day the oil light came on. In typical circumstances, that's a warning light, but for us, that was a signal of the end.

The mechanic informed us that the oil had become so full of sludge, that it destroyed the oil pump. The filter could no longer *filter*, the pump could no longer *pump*. It was like trying to drink a McDonald's milkshake through that little straw. The engine pretty much just dried up and the heat and friction became too much. It was over.

Here's the hardest part. All I had to do was a little bit of maintenance every 3,000 miles and this meltdown could've been avoided. All I had to do was pay attention to how much work the motor was doing and do my part to keep it in running order.

So, there I sat, in a cabin, *sluggish*, full of sludge, and slowing down, all because of my inability to do maintenance. Don't get me wrong, I read books, I took time to pray, time to study, even got away a little here and there. But I very rarely took time to do a full oil change.

What I had done was the equivalent of a full detail job while neglecting the heart, the engine that keeps it running. I had neglected to notice the oil light of my own soul coming on. I believed I could just keep on driving, mile after mile, and expect to run at high performance. I was pushing myself in ways that the human soul was not meant to be pushed.

My passion was pushing my emotional and physical RPMs into the red zone. My friends, *passion* is not engine oil. Our love for what we do doesn't keep the machine well-oiled. Sometimes, quite the opposite, *passion* can cause friction and damage, and before we know it, we just blow up.

Rebuild

My T-Bird suffered an untimely death and there was no way we could afford to rebuild the motor. It was too late. But what about me? What about my own inner engine that was heating up, on the verge of a burn out, because of my own neglect?

While at the cabin, I planned to sit and read a book and hear God scream something profound into my heart. Instead, he gave me that simple illustration of the oil change.

So, I prayed.

I asked God to flush out my heart. I prayed for a new *filter* for things to run through. The filter of seeing with His eyes, the filter of hearing with His ears. I want everything in life to run through HIS filter.

I prayed for a new *pump*. I want His heart to be *my* heart, His passion to be *my* passion, His motivation to be *my* motivation.

I prayed for fresh *oil*. I want to have that same fresh anointing I had when I first began. I want His vision to flow through my veins and reduce the friction and heat, that ministry can generate.

I prayed God would forgive me for my poor maintenance and teach me to see the warning lights before the meltdown.

I prayed that He would rebuild me from the inside out. I was ready to feel alive again.

The Sticker

We all know when they change your oil, you get a sweet new sticker on your window. It reminds you of when your next oil change is, so you'll be on top of it. It gives you the exact miles or date that you need to bring it back in and get maintenance done. It's great to have and takes the guesswork out.

Also, have you ever noticed that when you get your oil changed, it feels like the car runs better? In reality, you probably can't notice any difference at all, but it just *feels* better. You feel like you've accomplished something good and have been responsible. There's something comforting about knowing you have another several thousand miles ahead of you.

Here's the thing though. You get your oil done, feel good and drive off. But you have to go back... again and then again, and then again... maintenance is constant!

If you put 70,000 miles on a car and only do the maintenance once, you get a blown-up car. If you put years on your soul without some mental maintenance, you blow up your passion.

A cool keypad code thing on the door doesn't matter if the car won't run. No-one will want to steal it anyway. What good are comfy seats if it's just sitting in the junkyard?

We don't have a sticker. We don't have a reminder from the dealership, that it's time to do the scheduled maintenance on your heart.

We don't have a physical warning light that goes off to catch your eye and request immediate attention. We have feelings, that's it.

We begin to feel sluggish, slow, and unmotivated. Our passion begins to decline little by little. If we're not careful to pay attention to those signs, we may burn out and blow up.

You need a time-out

How do you do it? What does mental maintenance look like? Good news, it doesn't have to be a trip to Maui or a 2-week backpack through the mountains - unless that's what works for you, and you can afford it. It can actually be much simpler than that. Here's how I do it.

1. Take days off! I know this sounds dumb but do it.

Sometimes we allow ourselves to work non-stop because we feel if we don't, we're not being good stewards of our time and letting students down. Some feel it's a bragging right to be able to say, "Yeah, my job is never ending. Always on." WARNING! WARNING! CHECK ENGINE!

If you don't take at least one day to recover and rest, essentially, you're saying you can handle more than God Himself. I mean, we know the creation story in Genesis 2:2 *"By the seventh day God had finished the work he had been doing; so, on the seventh day he rested from all his work."*

The ancient Jewish culture was so dedicated to hard work that there had to be laws to take a day off. Laws! It's unhealthy to go, go, go. But hey, if you wanna work 24-7, knock yourself out. And that's exactly what you'll do.

2. Take a Sunday (or Wednesday) off. That one hurt, didn't it? I mean, a Saturday or even a Thursday is fine, but Sunday?

Who's gonna make sure things run the way they should? Who will teach the lesson or unlock the doors? Who's gonna make sure the pizza gets ordered? Your team!

If you master Chapter 7, you should be able to take a Sunday or two off, without worry or guilt. When you get to that place, you've matured as a leader.

I remember the first few times I was gone on a preaching day. I was literally watching the clock thinking, *Right now they should be starting worship time. I hope they remembered to turn on the speakers.* Or, *They're probably wrapping up by this point. I hope they remembered to make the announcements.* It was exhausting!

I found myself texting my team and asking if everything was going ok. I wasn't trying to micromanage, I just wasn't used to being away and having confidence in the team I had trained. But now when I'm gone... I'M GONE! I don't check in; I don't sneak away for a phone call. I trust that my team knows how we do things and I let them do those things!

We plan ahead and make sure all the bases are covered. Because of that, I can enjoy the time away with my family or whatever the thing is that has me away.

3. Take a vacation. I mean like multiple days away. For our family, we usually take a week around summertime and then another one around the holidays. In fact, as I write this, I am four days away from heading to a cabin in North Carolina to escape the Florida heat.

Here's the best part - I don't even have to worry about my team. While I'm gone, we won't hold our Sunday or Wednesday programs. Our kids will actually attend the adult service with their parents. Gasp! We do this a couple times a year.

For one, it's a great experience for kids to worship with the family, even if just once or twice a year.

Second, my team gets a break, too! Everyone gets to take a breath, hit reset, and come back fresh.

So, get away, even if it's to a local place, but far enough to not feel local. It doesn't have to be expensive or extravagant. It just has to be *away*.

4. Read Chapter 5 again. Clock out!

I'd love to wrap up this chapter with a story of how I was changed in the first couple days of the trip that I was talking about earlier. I'd love to tell you how I felt like a new man, ready to conquer the world with a fresh wind.

It didn't happen immediately. But I could sense my motor running better. I felt ready to go back and not only serve God with joy again, but I was ready to allow Him to refresh and renew my passion on a more consistent schedule.

Here's to maintenance and more miles ahead of you!

Matthew 28-30 (The Message) "Are you tired? Worn out? Burned out on religion? Come to me. Get away with me and you'll recover your life. I'll show you how to take a real rest. Walk with me and work with me—watch how I do it. Learn the unforced rhythms of grace. I won't lay anything heavy or ill-fitting on you. Keep company with me and you'll learn to live freely and lightly."

Chapter 11

COMPARISON KILLS

What I Wish I Knew When I Was New

Chapter 11
Comparison Kills

When I was a teenager, I was the most confident kid you've ever seen. I was always the smallest kid wherever I was (still the same as an adult), so I began to make up for it with my attitude. Whether it was music, a sport, bodybuilding, mullet growing, you name it, I was the best at it (at least in my own head).

I call it *confidence*, but let's be real; it's ego, pride, Napoleon Complex, Little-Man Syndrome. I actually wasn't even really that great at any of these things except the mullet one, but I had an ability to pick up on things quickly.

I was always a fast learner which made me feel like I was better than I really was. Whatever I got involved in, I would study. We didn't have the internet back in the day, so I learned from movies, shows, and magazines.

I would study Tom Cruise playing pool in The Color of Money.

I would study the bike tricks in the classic 80's movie Rad.

I'd be glued to the TV on Saturdays to learn from my favorite bowlers or buy every muscle magazine I could, to learn about growing the guns. I'd advance pretty quickly, and my ego would balloon.

I learned to bowl at a pretty impressive level rather quickly.

Starting at the age of 6, I played drums on stage with my Dad's band, without even doing rehearsals with them.

I could Bunny Hop my Kmart bike within a week of getting it, to impress the local gals.

Fast forward about 15 years, to my first couple of years in youth ministry. Let me remind you of Chapter 2. I was new, had zero experience, and no real desire to do youth ministry (I was just *helping* them at the time). I didn't grow up in a youth group, I never saw a youth group in action, and I could barely spell *youth group*.

But remember, I was a super quick learner. Why would youth ministry be any different? I got this! No problem!

Problem

What I actually learned, and pretty quickly; was, *I don't GOT this.*

I was lost in a giant, unfamiliar forest with no map or Uncrustables®. Sure, I had some of those early youth ministry books, which were really helpful, but there was so much to digest early on, that I didn't even know where to start.

Sidenote - If you're reading this book before you've read anything by Doug Fields, you're putting the cart before the horse! If you're not familiar with Doug... I'm sorry, Mr. Fields, he is the guru of our industry.

That guy has forgotten more about youth ministry than I'll ever know. I'm not telling you to stop reading this and start one of his, but please do yourself a huge favor and get anything he's put out there.

He even has marriage books where he and his wife Cathy... sorry, Mrs. Fields... have shared their wisdom with couples.

He's the Tom Brady, the Dale Earnhardt, and the Gordon Ramsey of student ministry. I digress, but it needed to be said.

Now where was I? Oh yeah; new and clueless.

A couple years in and I felt like I was drowning. Why wasn't I catching on to this like I did other things? Why didn't I feel like I was gaining knowledge and *succeeding*?

Here I was, put in charge of the spiritual lives of young people, which I *told* them was a bad idea to begin with, and I was really struggling. At least I felt that way.

Yes, we were slowly growing, and we all had a great time together, but I felt like I didn't have the depth of knowledge to move it along. I felt like I was robbing kids of a greater experience that they deserved from a youth pastor.

Where did this come from? Where was all of this doubt and angst coming from? Where was that confident 17-year-old who felt like he ruled the world? It came from the church down the street, and the one around the corner, and the one across town, and the one I read about in a book. At least that's what I told myself, but in reality, it came from my head and my own insecurities. I had become my biggest obstacle.

I'm not ashamed to admit this, well maybe just a little, but my struggles were really the product of jealousy. Yes, it's true that the jealousy came from my struggle of learning this ministry thing a lot slower than I imagined, but it was flat out envy. Period.

When I saw other youth groups that looked *better* than mine, it threw me into a funk. I tried to change, I swear I did, but I was so insecure. Everything I saw from another church made me feel even more insecure! Here's what I mean.

Real quick, let me clarify that this is different than the Community Playbook I talked about sharing. This isn't about wanting to learn from other people. This was about wanting what I didn't have. This is about the dangers of comparison.

Since our youth group met in a movie theater, this meant I couldn't really decorate or design a youth room. We had to get in there early, do a quick set up and hope everything was working by the time we let kids in. No fancy lights, no stage design, no play areas. Sure, the seats were really comfortable and had cup holders, but that wasn't quite the confidence-booster I needed.

Once, a local church was hosting a leadership conference and they were well-known and pretty big. As we arrived, we were able to tour their facility and of course, when I saw their youth area, I was instantly inspired and motivated. I was so excited for them and for what they were doing for young people in our community.

Just kidding, I was instantly deflated and discouraged. We didn't have a budget, much less a building! This place was less than a mile away from where we were meeting, and I knew I couldn't compete. No kid was gonna choose us over that! Would you pick Joe's Fun Park over Disney or your Uncle Dave's grilled box burgers over a Wendy's Baconator®? No! I was wasting my time!

That wasn't really true, but do you see what was happening there? I mean, I had no idea if their ministry was healthy, teaching bad theology, giving away free puppies, or anything. I knew *nothing* about them except that they were really popular and had a killer youth space, and I wasn't and didn't.

It was humbling and it was frustrating.

Here's another great example. Sometimes after our Wednesday night study group, we would drive one of the kids home. After dropping him off, the quickest way home was to pass another large and popular church. We would pass their parking lot about the same time their youth group was being released.

Every week, we would have an amazing study time, the kids were loving it, growing in their Bible knowledge, I was proud and happy. And can you guess what happened? We would pass that church, who had hundreds of teens in the parking lot and PSSSHHHHHH (that's the sound of deflation). My smile would disappear, my tone would change, and I was discouraged. All from passing a parking lot.

Again, I had no idea what they were doing in their ministry, and I wasn't mature enough to hope they were creating a fiery passion for Jesus. They had more kids; therefore, they were great, I was terrible.

Or how about this one? I took a trip to South Carolina to visit New Springs church. They had one of the fastest growing youth ministries in the US at the time, so I wanted to go check it out and learn some things.

I arrived early to their program, and we started my scheduled tour. I had my notepad, and I was eager to learn and ready to grow. They showed us some of their meeting spaces. They were pretty basic but decorated cool.

Cool logo and use the bright green color - check!

Then we went to one of their volunteer pre-service meeting areas.

Create a space for volunteer huddle meetings - check!

I was feeling pretty good at this point. But then... then their volunteers showed up. They had more volunteers running the check-in desk, than I had students in my whole ministry! PSSSHHHHH! You guessed it, deflated again.

Then after the volunteer meeting, it happened again. The students started showing up. I'd never seen so many kids in one place in my life. It was like stepping on an ant hill - they were coming from everywhere. They used the church's main adult auditorium because they couldn't fit them all in their old youth building. PSSSHHHHH! Are you seeing a pattern here?

The music portion was like something from a national conference, who had booked the greatest musicians on the planet. It was passionate, energetic, kids were jumping up and down and raising their hands. *Our kids stare at our band like they're singing in another language.* The lights and production were reminiscent of a live concert by

_____ (fill in your favorite performer). The message was powerful, and the speaker was so well polished. I don't need to make the sound again; you get the picture.

In truth, I was inspired. It was amazing and hey, they were 500 miles away from our church in another state. But yet, for some reason, my mental insecurities were still there. How was I ever going to do anything even close to this? I don't have the budget, the volunteers, the building, the knowledge, the blah, blah, blah.

Rather than focusing on the little things I could start adding or changing, I was too hung up on the overall scene that I saw, which was more than I could dare to think was ever possible; at least for little ole' me.

James, the half-brother of Jesus, warned us about this issue in his letter, Chapter 3, verse 16 (NLT)

> *"For wherever there is jealousy and selfish ambition, there you will find disorder and evil of every kind."*

I may not have stumbled into *evil*, but *disorder*? Absolutely. Comparing myself to organizations around me was affecting me in so many unhealthy ways. But my time was coming!

New building, same old brain.

Many, many years down the road, after building our

first facility and getting out of the movie theater, we built a youth center.

This thing was about to change my ministry forever! Indoor basketball court, video game center, meeting rooms, cafe with tons of candy and pizza and cheap Gatorades. Our new youth stage was almost as large as our old youth room! Now we had those fancy lights and a fog machine! 10,000 square feet of "Who's the big dog now?"

Finally, our time had arrived. We were about to attract hundreds if not thousands of new kids and introduce them to the Jesus we know and love. All of my notetaking and years of growing and learning was about to pay off.

However, yeah, here we go again, just a couple of months in, we had a revolt.

One student, who had been with us for years, started convincing a circle of friends that this new building was too big, not intimate, and personal like our small room.

That circle of friends bought in; they decided they didn't like the new music, the new lights, the new anything and some of them left our church. There was gossip, hurt feelings, parent meetings, and a chain of unrest that was killing the transition into *our dream come true.*

"But Earl, you gotta be mature enough to move past

these things and remember it happens in every church." You're right, but I wasn't. I took it all personally.

Now don't misunderstand me please. There is *nothing* wrong with big ministries, big production, or big budgets. But here's what I realized. I had to stop looking at what others were accomplishing because it made me miss what God was doing right in front of my own eyes.

The Good Stuff

I bought into the false notion that a large youth group means a healthy one. I had convinced myself that a bigger youth group meant a better youth group.

I remember one time chatting with Kurt Johnston who runs the middle school ministry at Saddleback Church in California. By the way, he's like Doug Fields... I mean, Mr. Fields. Buy his books, listen to his stuff. He's a genius.

He had mentioned a *low attendance* week at their usual youth service, during a holiday weekend. That number, for just middle schoolers, was literally 3 times the number of people in our whole church. I'm talking adults, kids, babies, teens, and babies counted again. But what he said has stuck in my head ever since and helped me to look at things with perspective. He said, "Big church, big youth group." AHHH! Got it!

Just about every church I had been comparing myself to, especially locally, was at least twice our size. This meant they also had bigger budgets, more volunteers, and more people to help them dream and create. I knew this, but I hadn't allowed it to be the lens I viewed things through.

Also, I had to think about the other side of the table. Imagine other youth leaders, still meeting in a movie theater or from a church much smaller than ours hearing me complaining about all of this. *Oh, I'm so sorry that your big new youth center isn't drawing the hundreds of kids for which you had hoped. I'm sorry your fancy lighting rig, that costs more than my yearly salary, isn't making two kids happy.*

I had forgotten what it was like in the beginning. I had strayed away from the very thing that kicked it all off; a passion to build relationships with kids and help them fall in love with Jesus.

I had forgotten that some of the greatest ministry moments for me, that produced the most fruit, were when we were at our smallest numbers, often not even in a dedicated youth room. I simply... just forgot.

It's ok to look around you. It's ok to be inspired by those with more experience and *more stuff*. You can learn a great deal that way; and be moved to take your ministry to new levels. But, don't be like me. Don't waste 3/4 of your career forgetting how God is using you and the resources *you do have*.

The kids that are showing up, are showing up because you have obviously offered them something the giant place down the road doesn't. Thank God for letting you play such a vital role in the lives of young people. It's not always about the lights or the cameras, but it *is* always about the action!

Proverbs 13:30 (NIV) "A heart at peace gives life to the body, but envy rots the bones."

Chapter 12

2 FEET A YEAR

What I Wish I Knew When I Was New

Chapter 12
2 Feet a Year

You've probably heard of a White Oak tree; they are found in much of North America. It can reach staggering heights at maturity, anywhere from 80-100 feet. That's impressive and all, but I learned something really interesting about them. A White Oak grows at the rate of 1-2 feet a year. That's it. So, in order for it to reach full maturity, it's gonna be awhile!

Do you like pears? I don't, but they fit the illustration here. Let's imagine that you do, and you wanted to grow your own pear tree. You're so excited! No more stores or fruit markets. Just walk out in the ole' yard and pick a few. Well, I hope you have some patience because from the time you plant it until the time it bears fruit, is around 4-6 years. Sorry. Maybe a peach tree is better. That one only takes 2-4 years.

It's important to know that youth ministry is very much like these trees. In my own experience, and others I know in our field, I didn't see growth or fruit for quite a long time.

Yes, there are kids you will see growing right before your eyes and you can tell they get it. But for the most part, this just isn't the case. There were so many times in my career when I wondered, a*m I making a difference at all or just wasting my time?*

A couple of months ago, a middle school boy came up to me after a service and said, "Great message today. That really hit home for me." I almost fell over! I can count on two hands how many times a kid has complimented my efforts. No, "Hey that retreat was so powerful. Thanks for putting all the effort into it." No, "Earl, I so appreciate that time you took taking me to breakfast and talking about my family life, and for picking up the bill."

It's not because they don't appreciate it, they're just kids. Unless you're a video game or the new Taylor Swift album, a teenager just doesn't show that much affection for things. Don't take it personally. They're not yet wired to show appreciation in a way we can gain momentum and confidence from.

Think about your own kids, or if you don't have any, ask a friend how many times their offspring say, "That dinner was amazing. Thank you for the hours of preparation." Or, "My clothes smell so clean. Thank you for making sure I'm always presentable." Again, it's not personal, it's just... kids.

It can be frustrating and steal your joy if you're the kind of person who needs validation. And there's nothing wrong with needing validation. Every *personality test* I've taken reminds me that I'm like a little child who needs to hear, "Great job, buddy. I'm so proud of you."

I don't need a test to tell me that, but it just confirms it. In fact, if you like this book, make sure to email me and tell me how much you enjoyed it. It'll fuel me for a long time! Just keep in mind, if validation is the only way you get motivated and jacked up; this may be a rough ride for you.

Now, parents may show you lots of love, which is priceless, but the kids will most likely show up and leave without patting you on the back, or your head if you're short like me.

One of my friends/volunteers and I were recently talking about this whole thing, and he made a great comparison, which sparked the idea for this chapter.

He said, and I paraphrase, "You don't plant a tree and climb it a week later. It takes a long time for the branches to mature." Brilliant! Keep that in mind when you pour countless hours into messages, events, lunch meetings, camps, and retreats, and not one kid gives you kudos.

You might hear remarks like, *that camp was awesome. I had so much fun,* but you might not. If they keep returning to your ministry, take that as a direct response to what you've put together. You may not get it face to face, but they are grateful for what you do. They really are.

How soon can you fix it?

When something we depend on breaks, we need it fixed immediately, if not sooner.

Here in Florida, there's a reason they call it "The Sunshine State," but that sounds way more friendly than it really is. From the months of June through October, it feels like our state sits on the sun. I mean it's like we have our own zip code and government *on the sun.*

No matter what you've heard about Florida, our greatest fear here is not alligators, or flying roaches, or tourists with their turn signal on for 6 miles. The thing that keeps you on edge is the lifespan of your air conditioner, whether it's in your house or your car. If that thing goes, get ready to experience a taste of a place we read about in our Bibles that Jesus warned us of.

When the sudden death of your air conditioning system occurs, you're on the phone immediately to find a repairman. When you get a hold of them, your first question isn't even about the cost, it's about how quickly they can fix it. You need it done yesterday!

Or consider your car. Most people have experienced a flat tire, which never comes at a convenient time. If you don't have a spare or can't change it yourself, we typically call roadside service. Again, our biggest question isn't usually, "How much will it cost," but rather, "How quickly can you be here?" We simply don't have time to wait on something to be fixed. We crave that instant resolution.

The thing is our profession is not like a car mechanic where kids come in broken and go home fixed.

Sometimes the "parts" take a while to come in. Sometimes a kid has to sit in our ministry for a long time before we start seeing progress or a significant turnaround. Sometimes we don't see that at all.

What happened?

I want to remind you that I'm speaking from my own experience and from my own personality. You may be way better at dealing with this, or anything that I've struggled with. I hope so. With that said, here's something I really wrestled with over and over.

When I saw "broken" kids in our ministry stay broken or lost kids stay lost, I felt like a failure. I say that in past tense, but it's just as real today as ever.

We can't help it. Our passion is to introduce young people to Jesus and watch their lives be altered in ways unimaginable. But when we've tried so hard for so long and that doesn't happen, it's hard to brush off.

Our hearts resonate so well with the story of the lost sheep in Matthew 18, where we leave the 99 to find the one, but we must remind ourselves of the other kids who ARE being impacted and changed.

The frustration may come when that same kid who was on his knees weeping at camp, hasn't shown up at church for months and his Instagram clearly shows why.

It may be the hour-long talk you had with a kid about not quitting school in his senior year, only to learn he never walked the stage at graduation.

It might be the girl that was a youth group superstar who graduated, not only from your youth group but from her faith. What happened? Was it me? Did I not do enough, say enough? Did I try hard enough to make it stick?

You did, my friend. You sure did.

You're a farmer

In these moments, one of the greatest lessons from our Bible is the parable of the seeds and soils. Check it out.

> *Matthew 13:3-8 (NIV) "Then he told them many things in parables, saying: "A farmer went out to sow his seed.*
>
> *4) As he was scattering the seed, some fell along the path, and the birds came and ate it up.*
>
> *5) Some fell on rocky places, where it did not have much soil. It sprang up quickly because the soil was shallow.*
>
> *6) But when the sun came up, the plants were scorched, and they withered because*

they had no root.

7) Other seed fell among thorns, which grew up and choked the plants.

8) Still other seed fell on good soil, where it produced a crop—a hundred, sixty or thirty times what was sown."

It's not you! It's such a common problem that Matthew found it necessary to record what Jesus said about it and make it available to us.

Every person in a faith journey falls into one of those soil categories. Some people simply take root quicker than others. Not every student you encounter is the same soil. Regardless, our job is to throw seeds. Lots of them! Over, over, and over.

When you're tired, throw seeds.

When you're frustrated, throw seeds.

When you're not sure one single kid is making any progress at all? Yep, keep throwing seeds!

Did you know that typically only 75-80% of corn that is planted actually germinates? It's less if the soil isn't right. But you don't see a farmer saying, "Why bother? A quarter of these won't even produce." They plant anyway. They do their best to prepare the field, secure a watering system, and rejoice in the harvest they get from it. Then they do it again next season.

We're farmers. Plant!

Remember when I was talking about cutting my grass and what a chore it was? Well, when my daughter was young, I planted three tiny oak trees in our yard on her birthday. They were so small that I ran two of them over with my mower because they blended in with the grass (which doesn't say much about my lawn care). One of them finally got big enough for me to keep it out from under the mower and it took off.

So, I only saw one-third of my "crop" mature. Not quite the harvest you'd brag about, but that one tree, over 15 years, grew mighty and strong and it was beautiful.

It's worth the wait

Don't forget verse 8 of the parable, it's important.

> *"Still other seeds fell on good soil, where it produced a crop—a hundred, sixty or thirty times what was sown."*

It took me over ten years before I started seeing some of the results of good soil.

When I started, my first wave of kids was on average about 15 or 16 years old. When some of them reached their mid-20's, I received my first *fruit basket* in the form of an email. It was from a young lady who told me how much she appreciated what my wife and I had done all those years, for her and her friends. She talked about the great memories she had growing up in our church and how she hopes they find a place like that for her kids one day in the future.

A few years later, another came from a young lady who had come to live with us for a month or so, while her family went through some difficult times. Her message talked about how she would have been lost without us, and what our love for the kids in our group means to her now that she's old enough to really understand it.

Just a few months ago, a young man who used to attend, now in his late 20's, stood in our living room. He was teary-eyed as he expressed his gratitude for us, and all of the support and love we had shown him and his family.

Those kinds of stories continually pop up, almost orchestrated by God for when I need them most. Those are the seeds we thought were being choked out, burned by the sun, or eaten by the birds.

But here's maybe the latest and greatest *fruit basket* I've experienced in the past few years. I'll let you read for yourself, an email I received just a few days ago.

> *"Hi Earl, I hope all is well, and I also hope you remember me. You have made a huge impact on my life and spiritual growth from*

8th grade, to now as an adult. I will always be grateful for experiencing my baptism, mission trips, and bible studies with you and your family. I have always felt the genuine love you and your family have shown. Even when we ran into each other at stores, you always made an effort to say "Hello." I hope you know those little gestures truly stuck with me and made me appreciate you as a person. I have recently moved to Dallas, TX and one of the best moments of my life is happening... I am getting MARRIED to a man who was heaven sent for me! I will be honored to have you marry me and my future husband. He knows how much this will mean to me and fully supports you marrying us. My faith in God is still forever strong and I know this will be another blessing to have you marry us.

I know!!! How cool, right? To this day I have done five weddings of former students, one was actually two students who met in our youth group, and I have 3 more scheduled in the next year.

I feel so honored they would want me to be part of the biggest day of their life.

And did you catch the first line of her email? *"I hope you remember me."* This is how much you will impact lives even if you don't realize it.

All of those stories are seeds that I planted long ago.

I may not have seen the growth right away or even before they left our group, but more seed falls on good soil then you'll probably ever know of.

It may take a White Oak 50 years to reach maturity and 4-6 years to get your pears, but how sweet it is when we stick around long enough to see it.

What I Wish I Knew When I Was New

Chapter 13

THE LONG HAUL

Chapter 13
The Long Haul

You may have heard this before, but the average *life expectancy* for a Youth Pastor at a given church is two and a half years. And by my observation, that period seems to be pretty accurate. From someone who's been in their position at the same church for 21 years, that's mind blowing to me.

I've actually seen this play out in churches in our own area, so many times. Remember the people I talked about who didn't want to share the love, or their strategies for youth ministry? Well, those people are long gone, and for some churches, many times over.

One of those churches I was so jealous of, actually went through four high school leaders in less than ten years. Three others went on to start their own church and become lead pastors. No thanks. I've seen that role and I don't have the capacity for that!

I'm not trying to be rude here, but if your goal is to do two years, learn from your Senior Pastor and then go start your own church, do the kids a favor and don't even start. I know that sounds mean even though I said I wasn't trying to be, so why would I say that?

Well, for many of these kids, especially a middle schooler, they don't have much consistency in their life. Their friend groups change, their teachers change, and their bodies are changing. For some, their families are changing in ways that are confusing and downright sad. Not much stays the same for them. We need to be an exception to that if at all possible.

Your consistency and dependability are the foundation for incredible ministry opportunities. Here's the biggest reason why.

It builds trust

Think about the person you trust the most. How long have you been a part of each other's life? Chances are it's been quite a while. In that time, you've learned a lot about each other.

You've learned how to interact with them, what they like and don't like. You know their strengths, weaknesses, family history, fears, worries, or what excites them the most. You not only know their favorite sports team, but their favorite player from that team. My point is, you trust them because you've spent enough time around them to verify, they're trustworthy. That's really hard to develop if you only spend two years with someone.

Please understand, I'm not saying you can't make a difference in that time frame. I'm not saying God doesn't put us in people's lives sometimes for a short duration.

I'm also not trying to shame anyone if their role ends not long after it began. Things happen. People move, get new opportunities, or maybe it's a health issue. My point is that in youth ministry, longevity opens up a huge door to walk through life with people because you've established deeper roots with those you come in contact with. They have learned that they can trust you.

By "they" I mean:

- **The Parents**

When I meet new parents, who are dropping their kids off in our room for the first time, one thing I always try to mention is how long I've been at the church. You can sense a little comfort when they hear that the church has let me stick around that long.

I also have parents who have already had kids come and go through our program. Now their youngest is part of the group and they feel at ease because we have history together over a long period of time.

I even have a boy in our group who is the first *2nd generation* kid. Yeah, his mom and dad met in my group and now have a kid in it! They would never stay at our church, much less let their son be in my ministry, if they didn't have that trust.

Sidenote - parents are not your enemy, despite what some youth workers like to say. Yes, some can be a nightmare, but that's the exception not the rule. Maybe I'll author another book all about that, depending on how this one goes.

- **The Students**

Imagine a kid who is going through something traumatic, or just heavy, and needing someone to talk to. Now imagine he or she is part of a youth group who has had 3 different youth leaders in the 4 years they've been there. I know there's exceptions to this, but chances are, that young person isn't going to spill their guts to someone they don't know, and who doesn't really know them either. For all they know, you're another stranger who will most likely be gone next year anyway. If they're going to trust you with the big stuff, they need to know they can count on you.

Our top priority isn't to preach messages, it's to build enough trust with those students that they know you're a go-to, solid, consistent person in their life. And that comes with time. Lots of time.

Relational ministry

This is a term that has become popular in youth ministry over the years, which is kind of weird to me. It's the idea that what we do is far more than just our programs, events, preaching, teaching, etc. The phrase implies that ministry should be relational, but isn't that the *only* kind of ministry? I mean, when I read through the Gospels and the rest of the

New Testament, that's where I see the biggest impacts.

Sure, Jesus did his share of teaching, and yes teaching is indeed a form of ministry, but it seems like the people who were most attracted to Jesus were drawn to Him because He was so relatable!

Andy Stanley has a saying we love to use in our church, "People who were nothing like Jesus, liked Jesus." He had a way of making people feel special and included, seen, and heard. And THAT opened the door for them to hear what He had to say.

In 1 Corinthians 9:19-23 (NIV), we see Paul, a genius, finding ways to be relational. Look at what he says.

> *"I am not anyone's slave. But I have become a slave to everyone, so I can win as many people as possible. When I am with the Jews, I live like a Jew to win Jews. They are ruled by the Law of Moses, and I am not. But I live by the Law to win them. And when I am with people who are not ruled by the Law, I forget about the Law to win them. Of course, I never really forget about the law of God. In fact, I am ruled by the law of Christ. When I am with people whose faith is weak, I live as they do to win them. I do everything I can to win everyone I possibly can. I do all this for the good news because I want to share in its blessings."*

He wasn't being a pushover and he wasn't a soft follower of Jesus, by any means. He just knew that in order to be effective, people had to feel like they had a connection with him.

There are groups of people today who would never step foot in our church for various reasons, but they might love hanging out with you at a birthday party. That's a start!

Becoming relational softens the edges of how some people view our faith.

Becoming relational shows people that you're willing to be in their life for the long haul.

It shows people that your interest in them is much more than a seat in the crowd for your sermon, and it creates a bond that even a great Bible study class can't generate. Here's a couple of personal examples I've experienced:

TJ started coming to our group in the 6th grade. We were always really close, so it was no surprise that we shared some special moments. I was there the day he got saved, I baptized him, we shared mission trips together, and became close with his family.

When he got into high school, he disappeared for a little while, but then eventually made his way back.

One of his good friends fell during football practice and had to have emergency brain surgery. It was pretty scary. During his recovery, I drove TJ to the hospital to visit his buddy. They got to hang out, listen to music, play some pool, and he shared his surgery wound with us, which TJ could really have done without.

Years later, it was TJ who called me to inform me of the sudden passing of one of our students, who was also his very best friend. In the moments of his own pain, he thought enough of our relationship to be the first to call me. We cried on the phone together and walked through that grief side by side.

Today, TJ serves on my adult team. He gives sermons and is the main leader of our high school boys small group, as well as other things. That doesn't happen without relational ministry. Those moments gave him a reason to stick around.

Megan leads our worship team. She's in her mid-20's and also started in our ministry in the 6th grade. I'm performing her wedding in a few months.

Three people on that worship team are kids who graduated many years ago. Two of them are brothers who I spent a lot of time with when their father was shipped overseas, to serve our country for a couple of years. Oh, and their dad came back home and guess what? He now serves with us as a middle school small group leader and service host.

Lacey, my youngest daughter, is now married and grown up. She grew up in our church, so if anyone would want to escape the ministry world it's a Pastor's kid. But... she is my volunteer coordinator, runs high school girls' small groups, trains small group leaders, and plans events.

I've had kids ask if I can sit with them at the hospital before a surgery or if I would come see them after their suicide attempt.

I've had a kid ask if I would ride in the car with him on the way to his father's funeral.

I've had a kid ask his parents if I could come with them when they picked him up from jail (probably a smart move, having the Pastor in the car during the ride home). He then spent hours with us at our house talking about his decision-making skills.

I haven't had a kid name their baby after me yet, but maybe "Earl" isn't a great first choice anyway.

Why does this happen? Relational ministry.

Go to their games, concerts, or plays. Text and ask how their Mom's surgery went and send a meal to them if you can. Keep checking in to ask them how they're doing after their big breakup. Make a big deal out of their big (or small) accomplishments. Send them a handwritten card when they get their driver's license or braces off. *These are the moments they remember far more than a sermon you spent all week on.*

This is where you prove that you're not pretending to like them just so they'll show up at your stuff and you can count them in your attendance numbers.

This is what makes them invite you to their graduation, perform their wedding, name their kids after you. *Maybe not the last one.* I really need to get over that.

These are the times where the foundation is laid for you to pour Jesus into them, not just from the stage, but in real, every day, sometimes extremely hard, life.

Relationally ministry not only changes them, but it mimics the very strategy of Jesus Himself. Being relational is risky because it will require your time, your efforts, and your emotions. But if Jesus was willing to go there, then so will I.

What I Wish I Knew When I Was New

Conclusion

Conclusion

Conclusion

I know this book may have been a little heavy in parts, but that's what I found ministry to be at times... heavy.

Two decades ago, I agreed to take the job with the candy-coated anticipation of pizza, games, some Jesus stuff, and a bunch of kids who thought I was the coolest guy in church (which I wasn't).

I went in with the expectations that my little rip-and-read lessons and a couple of bounce house events a year, would cover the gamut of my job role. There were so many things that I never expected and some I never wanted. There were so many things I wasn't prepared for that didn't fall into the "fun and feel good" category. But, to be honest, I wouldn't have it any other way.

If youth ministry were all about lock-in's, pizza parties and *all hail the mighty youth leader*, I'd bow out. Sure, it would be easier and flattering but, I don't want that kind of shallow, meaningless, candy-coated calling for my life.

Jesus didn't say, "Come to me all who are lookin' for a good time, a cool youth room and a soda chug contest!" He dealt with those who were messed up, heartbroken, hopeless, and helpless. He dove in headfirst to a pool of sinful, disobedient, stubborn people, that He chased after when they were drowning in the deep end. Matthew 9:36 reveals why, compassion.

> *"When He saw the crowds, He had compassion on them because they were confused and helpless, like sheep without a shepherd."*

It's one of the things that makes us most like Jesus. In fact, it makes us *a lot* like Him. I'm pretty positive Jesus had some sleepless nights as His heart broke for those He encountered.

I'm sure He sat and thought about the destructive choices even some of His closest followers were making. But compassion propelled Him forward. Compassion fueled His ministry. Compassion made it all bearable. Compassion was the backbone of why He chose to endure death on our behalf.

Sometimes compassion is messy and emotional and pushes us to places we never knew we could reach. But compassion, in its most sincere form, is really just love. Jesus wasn't caught off guard by this kind of love He would have for people, and I don't want you to be either.

I'm praying for you as you dive into the youth ministry pool and begin your journey. Splashing around in waist-high water is fun but you're called to the other side where it's deep, dangerous, and tempting to stay away from. Compassion is the life preserver you will be called to throw out time and time again. Be ready, be willing. Take a deep breath... and jump!

PS, If you ever need someone to talk to or ask advice from, I'd love to be one of those people. I'm no expert, but I've sure learned a thing or two over the years.

AuthorEarlHenning@gmail.com

www.ingramcontent.com/pod-product-compliance
Lightning Source LLC
LaVergne TN
LVHW051836080426
835512LV00018B/2913